GEMS FROM SOLOMON

GEMS FROM SOLOMON

A study on love and marriage
through Solomon's life and writings

With Commentaries on *Proverbs 31*
and *The Song of Solomon*

Ronald C. Surels, Ph.D.

To LYNNE

*My caring and loving companion
who is my true 'soulmate' and
fulfills her calling of wife and mother
with love, grace, and distinction.*

Some Advice From Solomon's God-given Wisdom

"My son, if you receive my words, and treasure my commands within you, so that you incline your ear to wisdom and apply your heart to understanding;... If you seek her as silver, and search for her as for hidden treasures; then you will understand the fear of the Lord, and find the knowledge of God." (Proverbs 2:2,4-5)

"Happy is the man who finds wisdom, and the man who gains understanding; for her proceeds are better than profits of silver, and her gain better then fine gold. She is more precious than rubies, and all the things you may desire cannot compare with her." (Proverbs 3:13-15)

"How much better to get wisdom than gold! And to get understanding is to be chosen rather than silver." (Proverbs 16:16)

"Live joyfully with the wife whom you love all the days of your vain life which He has given you under the sun, all your days of vanity; for that is your portion (reward) *in life, and in the labor which you perform under the sun." (Ecclesiastes 9:9)*

CONTENTS

INTRODUCTION

The purpose of this book is an attempt to present a broader understanding of love, marriage, and relationships through the character of one of the wisest men that ever lived—King Solomon of Israel. It is not an epistle of his entire life, nor does this study cover the myriad of wisdom principles that the Lord our God bestowed upon him. This little book seeks to bring a deeper understanding not only of Solomon himself but also his insightful *wisdom* on love and marriage. His writings of Scripture contain a wealth of Godly insights from which we can mine a few gems concerning our subject matter. To do this we delve deeply into the Hebrew language, culture and concepts to examine some details of his life concerning his "loves" and frustrations through what he has written (as led by the Holy Spirit) about his experiences and conclusions. Solomon was guided by the Holy Spirit to write three of the books that make up our Holy Bible: *Proverbs*, *Ecclesiastes*, and *The Song of Solomon*. Because of his humble character in asking not for himself but for his people, he was to soon reign over; God also granted him wisdom, power, and riches. In a deeper examination of his writings, we can review some important truths concerning the subjects cited above, as well as a deeper understanding of Solomon himself. Indeed, this book is written on the premise that in Solomon's wisdom and experience, we can refresh ourselves with some of these "gems" of truth that God has provided to enhance our life and His will in our lives. If we believe that the scriptures are infallible and divinely inspired (authored) by God—as Jesus proclaimed, *"For assuredly, I say to you, till heaven and earth shall pass away, one jot or one tittle will by no means pass from law till all is fulfilled (Matthew 5:18)—* then we can believe that everything that the writers, prophets, and others who are in the Bible said—and did—is and of the Truth. The scriptures testify to God's oversight and direction: *"All scripture is given by inspiration of God, and is profitable for doctrine, for reproof, for correction, for instruction in righteousness, that the man of God may be complete, thoroughly equipped for every good work" (2 Timothy 3:16-17)*; and *"For the word of God is living and powerful, and sharper than any two-edged sword, piercing even to the division of soul and spirit, and the joints and marrow, and is a discerner of the thoughts and intents of the heart." (Hebrews 4:12)*.

Solomon wrote many proverbs and songs—one thousand five songs and three thousand proverbs, according to Josephus, the ancient Jewish historian; one-third of which he included in his Scriptural writings. The book of *Proverbs,* which teaches much of what God bestowed upon him, as well as of what his father David had taught him, is replete with wisdom. (If parents center the upbringing of their children on the book, it can endow them for much better success in life. The same applies for schools in their teaching curriculum.)

The book of *Ecclesiastes,* written later in his life, is his "confessional"—how he tried just about everything in life but all of it brought no lasting satisfaction. And then there is *The Song of Solomon*, the book that many wonder why it is even in the Bible, let alone try to make some sense of it. It is so full of Hebraic cultural phrases and idioms that unless one has studied that ancient culture, very little understanding, and edification can be received from it. When correctly interpreted, as is attempted here, the book reveals deep and beautiful truths concerning commitment, purity, faithfulness, and love. Assigning the characters to their proper roles in this poetic epistle, beautiful analogies concerning God, the Believer, and the World can be constructed in both Hebrew and Christian religious cultures.

When we examine Solomon's writings as a whole, we can better understand what kind of a man Solomon was, the forces that exist which seek our allegiance, and the sacredness of human and Godly love. That is more than enough for this small book to try and cover. *The Song of Solomon* and the verses of *Proverbs 31* are presented in 'verse-by-verse' commentary, using the Hebraic language and concepts to shed light on the subject matter. The rest of *Proverbs* and the book of *Ecclesiastes* by themselves, because of their length and the entailment of many ancient Hebraic idioms and the like, are not presented in full 'verse-by-verse' commentary. Certain verses, however, are cited from these scriptures to gain a better understanding of Solomon and his teaching. There are also a few chapters that delve further into the subjects of love and marriage, which hopefully not only help us to understand Solomon and his dilemma but provide God's truth in these areas, something sorely needed in our culture today.

This book is centered in the Old Testament. It is this portion of the Bible upon which everything else in the Scriptures is based. The beginnings (Creation), history of God's chosen people, the Messianic prophesies of the coming Messiah, the Law of God, and His principles concerning life and morality are all found here. Several passages of the Old Testament were quoted and used in their teachings by Jesus Christ and writers in the New Testament. As Solomon wrote, "*...there is nothing new under the sun*" (*Ecclesiastes 1:9c*). All of our modern Western culture's principles, morals, law—and even basic human characteristics found the world over—stem from the Old Testament. Just to name a few— on the human heart: *"The heart is deceitful above all things, and desperately wicked; who can know it? (Jeremiah 17:9);* on God's unchanging redemptive actions: *"If My people who are called by My name will humble themselves, and pray and seek My face, and turn from their wicked ways, then I will hear from heaven, and will forgive their sin and heal their land (2 Chronicles 7:14).* This is just as true today through the saving blood of Jesus Christ for us on the cross. The New Testament book of Hebrews states that *"…without the shedding of blood there is no remission of sins" (Hebrews 9:22b).* The blood sacrifice needed changed from animals to a man—God Himself in the flesh. God is the same, He does not change, and we can trust that. There are different times—*dispensations*—in which He does things differently as His people and culture mature, but the principles remain the same. The Old Testament principle truths are just as applicable in New Testament times today as before. Hence Solomon's Godly wisdom, as revealed in ancient times, is as up-to-date for humanity as tomorrow's newspaper.

The following people have been a great assistance in helping me prepare this manuscript for printing: Lynne, my dear sweet wife—truly my 'soulmate,' sacrificing some of our time together, and encouraging with her insightful suggestions (we celebrate 50 wonderful years of our marriage this year of the book's publication); my beautiful granddaughter Rachel Ballard (a talented young writer whom I hope to see published in the near future); and our dear friend Lesley Gore, whose expertise in proofreading has also been most appreciated. To have them reviewing the manuscript and offering suggestions has been extremely beneficial and helpful towards making this book a reality.

For the best enjoyment and learning experience, it is suggested that this book be read **slowly** and with a Bible beside you for a referral to the Scriptures cited. This work is **not** so much a "devotional"—rather, it is a **deeper study** into the very Word of God. As we are urged in *Hebrews 6:1* to press on to maturity in our faith, I pray this work will bring deeper insights into Scripture to help in our lives on the subjects covered.

In *2 Timothy 2:15,* we are encouraged to **study** to prove ourselves **diligent** in giving forth the Word, the thought being so that we can grow deeper in the Lord—and, as has we hopefully surmise, dig out the gems—that our Lord God placed there for us. The Bible has the answers to all of our questions in life. To "search the Scriptures" (*John 5:39*; *Acts 17:11*) and seek to comprehend in our study some of the Solomonic wisdom that lie within is to hopefully grow into discovering more of the mind and purpose of God for our lives, for our world. It is my prayer that this little book will help us to do just that.

—Ron Surels, Ph. D.

ONE

Solomon the Man

Solomon was a young man barely in his 20s, very tall and handsome when he was appointed the king of Israel after his father, King David's death. This was according to the instruction of God and his father's wishes, as David relayed to Bathsheba, mother of Solomon: *"Just as I swore to you by the LORD GOD of Israel, saying, 'Assuredly Solomon your son will be king after me, and he shall sit on my throne in my place, so I certainly will do this day.'"* *(1 Kings 1:30)*. Adonijah, the fourth son of David, and older than Solomon, thought that he should rule after his father's death, and so made himself king. Nathan, the prophet, and Solomon's mother, Bathsheba, went to David and advised him of Adonijah's attempt to usurp the throne. Hearing this, David immediately decreed that his son Solomon should be King and made it so. (*1 Kings 1:1-35*). And so Solomon became king of Israel for 40 years—the wisest and richest ruler the world has known. His wisdom has resonated down through the centuries. Just one example is his advising quick justice on criminal acts: *"Because the sentence against an evil work is not executed speedily, therefore the heart of the sons of men is fully set in them to do evil" (Ecclesiastes 8:11)*—an important truth that our society should encompass today more than it does.

Solomon started out so wonderfully bestowed with glory and honor—only to end up personally frustrated and unhappy. We probe why this was so and how one might avoid falling into what he did—a life of 'vanities,' the subject of his book of *Ecclesiastes*.

TWO

Solomon the King

On the threshold of the beginning of his forty years as King of Israel, God gave Solomon a promise:

"At Gibeon the Lord appeared to Solomon in a dream by night; and God said, "Ask! What shall I give you?" (*1 Kings 3:5*). This was an open-ended statement suggesting that *anything* Solomon asked for would be his. At this 'carte blanche' offer, Solomon looked in <u>four directions</u>:

1. **Back** to his father's reign: *"And Solomon said: 'You have shown great mercy to Your servant David, my father, because he walked before You in truth, in righteousness, and in uprightness of heart with You; You have continued this great kindness for him, and You have given him a son to sit on his throne, as it is this day."* (*1 Kings 3:6*);

2. **Within** himself to see his inadequacy: *"Now, O Lord my God, You have made Your servant king instead of my father David, but I am a little child; I do not know how to go out or come in."* 1 Kings 3:7);

3. **Out** over the multitude of people he was to rule: *"And Your servant is in the midst of Your people, too numerous to be numbered or counted."* (*1 Kings 3:8*);

4. And finally, **Up** to God to request help: *"Therefore give to Your servant an understanding heart to judge Your people, that I may discern between good and evil. For who is able to judge this great people of Yours?"*(*1 Kings 3:9*). This pleased God that he did not ask for selfish things but for understanding and discernment

17

so that he could rule well. God honored his requests by giving him **more** than what he asked for—riches and honor in addition to wisdom: *"The speech pleased the Lord, that Solomon had asked for this thing. Then God said to him: 'Because you have asked this thing and have not asked long life for yourself, nor have asked riches for yourself, nor have asked the life of your enemies, but have asked for yourself understanding to discern justice, behold, I have done according to your words; see, I have given you a wise and understanding heart, so that there has not been anyone like you before you, nor shall any like you arise after you. And I have also given you what you have not asked: both riches and honor so that there shall not be anyone like you among the kings of all your days. So if you walk in My ways, to keep My statutes and My commandments, as your father David walked, then I will lengthen your days."* (*1 Kings 3:10-13*). Solomon begins his reign revealing his God-given wisdom as recorded in *1 Kings 3:16-28*—the well-known episode of two women each claiming to have given birth to the same baby. His fame with riches and honor grew throughout all Israel and beyond, even unto other nations: *"So Solomon reigned over all kingdoms from the river to the land of the Philistines, as far as the border of Egypt. They brought tribute and served Solomon all the days of his life"* (*1 Kings 4:21*).

Beginning in his early adult life, Solomon, with celerity, expanded the influence of Israel throughout the area as well as building up his own possessions and lifestyle. His reign, based upon what his father David did and taught him, but especially the gifts of wisdom and prosperity from God, is historically noted as an example of one of the best, if not *the* best, reigns ever. He seemed to be the perfect king, loving and serving the Lord, ruling in wisdom, performing great projects such as building God's house (temple), the walls of Jerusalem, and his own magnificent house.

But as he grew, his weaknesses became apparent and began to rule in his life. Paramount was his love for women and liquor. Early in the reign, his mother, Bathsheba, saw these weaknesses and passionately warned him, as recorded in *Proverbs 31* (described in the next chapter). In his "love" for *hundreds* of women, he allowed their gods and worship of such to be in his kingdom. *"But King Solomon loved many foreign women, as well as the daughter of Pharaoh...(and) from the nations of whom the Lord had said to the children of Israel, 'You shall not intermarry with them nor they with you. Surely they will turn away your hearts after their gods. Solomon clung to these in love. And he had 700 wives, princesses, and 300 concubines; and his wives turned away his heart."* (*1 Kings 11:1-3*). Note that the verse cited states that "*...Solomon clung to these in love...*" The word "clung" (cleaved) in Hebrew is '*dabaq*'—'to pursue hard, hold fast; to cling; to pursue; to seek earnestly, frantically.' The concept here is that he **desperately** held fast to these foreign women in love relationships, seeking to find a true "soulmate," his special or "specific woman." These women mentioned in *1 Kings 11:1* were *strange* (foreign) women from various tribes and nations in a large area around Israel who were serious about practicing their pagan religions, with whom Solomon entered into marriage relationships. He forged a political alliance with the Pharaoh of Egypt via the Pharaoh's daughter (*cf.1 Kings 3:1*), and then several other foreign women who at least in part entered into a similar kind of political marriage with Solomon. He had many women around him, living in a polygamous situation. He no doubt believed that by doing so, it would help extend and influence the wealth and peace of his kingdom—which it did. Concubines were other women he kept for his erotic purposes. These women were highly influential, and he was so easy going that he granted them their religious practices. They apparently did not have much trouble in turning Solomon toward their false gods and away from the Lord God of Israel: *"For it was so, when Solomon was old, that his wives turned his heart after other gods; and his heart was not loyal to the Lord his God, as was the heart of his father David…So the Lord became angry with Solomon, because his heart had turned away from the Lord God of Israel…"* (*1 Kings 11:4,9*).

Much later in life, reflecting on what David, his father, taught him while he was very young, he includes some of these fatherly teachings in his writing of *Proverbs,* such as the one that says: *"Keep your heart with all diligence, for out of it spring the issues of life"* (*4:23*). He no doubt thought back—with much regret—on his earlier life in which he did not *"keep his heart in all diligence"* and completely heed his father's advice. Being a humble man and inspired by God, he shares the failures and frustrations of his life in his *Song of Solomon,* and especially in *Ecclesiastes.* His writings reveal that he was intensely searching for the **right** woman for him.

The result of how Solomon fared in the search for his "soul-mate" among all his women will be dealt with in detail in the following chapters.

THREE

The Legacy of Bathsheba

The book of *Proverbs*, authored by Solomon and, as stated earlier, includes much of what his father, King David, taught him. In the last chapter,—*31*—the first nine verses record what Solomon's mother Bathsheba taught him, and she *may* have also authored the rest of the chapter which Solomon wrote down. (This all could be called the 'Legacy of Bathsheba,' as suggested by some and adopted as the title of this chapter.)

Bathsheba recognized his weaknesses and was alarmed and frustrated enough to earnestly admonish him three times: "*The words of King Lemuel, the utterance which his mother taught him: What, my son? And what, son of my womb? And what, son of my vows? Give not your strength to women, nor thy ways to that which destroys kings. It is not for kings, O Lemuel, it is not for kings to drink wine, nor for princes intoxicating drink: Lest they drink and forget the law, and pervert the justice of all the afflicted."* (*Proverbs 31:1-4.*) These opening verses of *Proverbs 31* introduce the mother of Solomon and her very intense utterance to her son, the king. In Hebrew, the word used for her speaking is '*massa*' (from the root '*nasa*') meaning "an utterance, to loudly proclaim." (It can also refer to a statement of doctrine to be taught.) The word "taught" in Hebrew is '*japar*,' to correct; chastise; reprove. These words reveal Bathsheba's frustration and deep concern for her son as she recognizes that he is going in an opposite direction in life, looking for fulfillment in the wrong places. Bathsheba loudly laments his actions in trying to convince Solomon of his folly! In verse two, the three "*whats*" spoken in desperation to Solomon by his mother, are a triple interrogative revealing the severe intensity of her concern as he is about to assume the throne. Bathsheba was a very intelligent woman (notwithstanding her participation in sin with David), as evidenced in her alliance with the prophet Nathan when they prevented Adonijah's conspiracy from usurping Solomon, who was the rightful heir, of his kingship (see *1Kings*, especially *1:11-30*).

The Hebrew word for king in *Proverbs 31:1* is '*melek*' and prominently indicates that the author of this chapter section *is* the king who is named "*Lemuel*." This looks like a proper name, but in Hebrew, it is not. The word is two prepositional phrases, convoluted with a noun. The first part of the name is the preposition '*lem*' that should be translated "unto him" and the second *('la') 'u-el'* means "unto (belonging to) God," so literally in Hebrew the word "*Lemuel*" means "unto him, unto God." It is not a pronoun. There never was a king named 'Lemuel' either in secular or religious history. The accurate translation of the verse would be: "T*he words of the king, unto him who belongs to God"; or "The words of a king, belonging to God."* This, then, is simply another name or title for Solomon.

Solomon continues with the complaint of his mother, revealing how she tries to teach or admonish him to refrain from two things: womanizing and liquor. In verse 3, the word "strength" in Hebrew is '*chayil*' which means '**virtue.**' It's the same Hebrew word that is used in the 10th verse for 'virtuous.' The concept here is that virtue enables moral strength and moral strength also enables virtue—in other words, they go hand-in-hand—inner strength of character that produces virtue, and virtue enables one to be morally strong of mind and purpose, which in turn determines physical activities or lifestyle. The Hebrew word "*ways*" in verse 3 is '*dherekh' (derek)*, and although this Hebrew noun can mean a 'path,' 'road,' 'journey,' 'way of life' (lifestyle) for example, in the context here and in other scriptures (such as *Jeremiah 3:2 & 13)*, the word means 'sexual favors.' And the phrase 'strange women' (Heb. *'zur'*) has to do with 'different' or 'adulteress' women.

Bathsheba believes that Solomon's lifestyle—especially concerning women—will give him serious problems in his reign as king and will affect even the nation.

And this is exactly what happens when he continues to allow false gods and pagan worship through his many wives, as seen in *1 Kings 11:9-11*: *"And so the Lord became angry with Solomon, because his heart had turned from the Lord God of Israel, who had appeared to him twice, and had commanded him concerning this thing, that he should not go after other gods, but he did not keep what the Lord commanded. Therefore the Lord said to Solomon, 'Because you have done this, and have not kept My covenant and My statutes, which I have commanded you, I will surely tear the kingdom away from you and will give it to your servant.'"*

Even though he did not take his mother's advice, he realized much later that she was right.

Solomon never obtained what he thought was his "special woman"—for which he sought desperately. The following chapters discusses the concept of what is meant by a "special woman" and Solomon's failure and his "confession" in the pursuit of such.

FOUR

The *'Proverbs 31'* Woman
A Commentary

The book of Proverbs closes by describing the ideal Godly wife. *Proverbs 31:10-31* is an *acrostic* in that each of the 22 letters of the Hebrew alphabet is used in sequence to begin the first word of each verse. As such, each meaning of the first **letter** is presented indicative to the object or principle defining the letter, which in turn gives meaning to the word and then to the verse. Each verse shown here will begin in sequence with the appropriate letter from the present Hebrew alphabet and the Paleo (ancient) Hebrew letter if different, followed by the English *transliteration* letter, the *transcription* (phonetic) if needed; then the Paleo Hebraic *pictograph definition* of the letter, and finally the verse itself outlined in italics, followed by a commentary as to its meaning and purpose.[1] (All the following verses are from *Proverbs 31*.)

31:10—*ALEPH, ALEF-* 'a' *(ah)*—ox; strength; gentle: *"Who can find a virtuous wife? For her worth is far above rubies."* A virtuous wife is a woman who is capable in leading the domestic duties of the household of her husband. The verse could also be literally translated as: "A woman of capacity (ability), who can find? To find such a woman for a wife is to find something—or someone—far more valuable than jewels." We could perhaps even say in our vernacular that she would be 'worth her weight in gold.'

---

1 In the original Hebrew language, every Hebrew letter is a sound, a word, and a picture, which all fit together to have meaning.

A *pictograph* is a pictorial sign or symbol (like Egyptian hieroglyphics); *transliteration* is the process of mapping letters from one alphabet into another alphabet using *graphology* (letter shapes); *transcription* is the process of matching the *sounds* of speech to letters. (cf. A chart is in the Appendices to help understand this section.)

She would be solid in morals and values, gentle and creative. In her character are strong mental, emotional, and spiritual traits that her husband needs. It was God's intention when he created man and woman is that the woman was to be a **helper** or **help meet** for him. The last part of *Genesis 2:18* shows God saying, *"I will make him a **helper** comparable to him."* Literally, "a helper like him" or "fit for him"—the word combination "soulmate" fits this perfectly, truly a symbiotic relationship. (A deeper explanation of "soulmate" follows in Chapter 5.)

31:11—*BETH, BEYT*—'b'—family; tent or house; inside: *"The heart of her husband safely trusts her; so he will have no lack of gain."* She responds so completely to him that he is confident of her steadfast loyalty. She watches over all that he has and helps him gain prosperity. She is always there for him—her whole being is centered in him and no other man.

Because she takes such good care of him, her husband does not have to look elsewhere for anything, which is the meaning of the phrase *"…no lack of **gain**"* (Heb. *shalal- shaw-lawl*= to take spoil; a purpose.) They truly have a "one flesh" marriage—again, a symbiotic relationship.

31:12—*GIMEL*—'g'—foot; a camel; gather; walk: *"She does him good and not evil all the days of her life."* (Heb. *tob* =deal bountifully; to cause good.) She will bring him blessings and never purpose to trouble him in any way. Her main goal in life is to continually (…"*all the days of her life"*) assist and bless him; having an attitude of him being her earthly "lord", as Sarah had with her husband (compare *1 Peter 3:6*). This, unfortunately, does not sit well with the modern woman in our Western culture of today. Many erroneously think that to be submissive to a man in any way is akin to slavery or at least not being their own independent person. But in God's creative, act He designed the woman to find fulfillment in the man, and he in turn finding fulfillment in the woman as he gives forth his love to her. In other words, it is the symbiotic relationship in which both give and receive; and when done right and proper according to God's principles, it is as Solomon says, "*...a good thing*" (*Proverbs 18:22*), and the greatest and best you can achieve in life (the implication of *Ecclesiastes 9:9*).

31:13—*DALETH, DALET*— 'd'—door; a path; a way of life; right movement: "*She seeks wool and flax, and willingly works with her hands.*" This refers to decisions (going to the right 'door,' making proper decisions to follow). In every task, she has her husband in mind as well as the entire household. She carefully shops (Heb. *darash* =to diligently search) for the right materials, such as wool for cold weather, flax for warm to make appropriate clothing, and she does so with pleasure (Heb. *chephets—k-hay'-fets* =delight; desire, willingness).

31:14—*HEH, HE, HEY*— 'h' 'eh'—behold; to show; window; reveal: " *She is* like *the merchant ships, she brings her food from afar.*" Here is an indication that she has a propensity for business, something like an importer, or she may be buying from a person or business that imports food from other countries. The phrase "*She is...*" (Heb. *hayah*—haw-yaw =to become like; similar)—is analogous in describing her extra effort of buying properly (verse 16) in order to prepare good food for her family. She is particular and chooses her food with discretion, and like the merchants, delivers (transports) the food she has carefully chosen to her house. As the merchants bring goods that they know the people will want, so she brings (Heb. *bow'bo*=bring forth) home good food that she knows her husband enjoys and is nutritious for all.

31:15—*VAW, VAU, VAV*—'u' ' ooh' 'v' or 'w'—secure; nail; peg; joining together; bind: "*She also rises while it is yet night, and provides food for her household, and a portion for her maid-*

servants." She is one who is a basic mainstay to the household and holds it together. *"She also rises…"*(Heb. *qum*—koom= rise to accomplish; to perform) indicates a task that is needful. She gets up before anyone else in her household and oversees breakfast. She may or may not actually do the work, but she sees to it that everybody is fed. The word *"**portion**"* (Heb. *choq*— *hoke* =commandment; statute; task) indicates that she gives her maid-servants instructions. She does this joyfully, working to help provide order and stability in the home.

 31:16—*ZAYIN, ZAIN*—'z'—a sword; axe; weapon; cut; pierce; plan:*" She <u>considers</u> a field and buys it, from her profits she plants a vineyard."* The Hebrew letter for this word actually signifies **aggressiveness**. This definitely shows that in addition to her domestic talents, she is also a businesswoman. She *"considers"*(Heb. *zamam*—zaw-mam' to plan; think it through;) and then buys a field, contracts some kind of a business deal where she gains capital; and with it, she continues her business ventures by planting a vineyard. She is an aggressive, intelligent businesswoman, but it is all for her husband and their household. (Principle: There are wives who are the more domestic type and others who are the more business type, but all can do both to a greater or lesser degree.)

 31:17—*CHETH, CHET*- strength; wall; separation: *"She girds herself with strength, and <u>strengthens</u> her arms."* She has strength of character, which reflects forward to the phrase *"strengthens her arms"* (Heb. *amats*—aw-mats—to be alert; make strong; and *zroa*- *zroah*—stretch out the arm; to help), meaning that she is protective and alert to needs of her husband, household, and even to people outside the home. She is ever ready to assist and help out wherever she can and knows how to keep things in order.

31:18—*TETH, TET*—'t' 'th'—to coil; surround; a basket: "*She perceives that her merchandise is good, and her lamp does not go out by night.*" She understands that what she does is work that lasts—"*does not go out by **night***"—(Heb. *layil, laylah*—of light; adversity) and she will complete her tasks and not leave them unfinished; difficulties do not stop her—she perseveringly moves on. She surrounds herself with singleness of purpose for every task.

31:19—*JOD*, YOD—'y' 'i' 'eeh'—arm with closed hand; work; deed; worship: "*She stretches out her hands to the distaff, and her hand holds the spindle.*" Her hands are an extension of her soul (character), which, being centered around her husband, keeps her eagerly tending to the needs of her household. She is not out running around trying to please or impress people. The spindle and distaff are analogous to order, direction, and purpose, involving her domestic chores. The phrase "*stretches out her hands*" (Heb. *shalach*—*shaw-lakh*—send out; reach forth) shows that her helping arms reach out not only to her household but also into the neighborhood, as seen next.

31:20—*CAPH, KAPH, KAF*—'k'—palm of open hand; bend; allow; cover: "*She extends her hand to the poor, yes she reaches out her hands to the needy.*" Being comfortable with her husband and the household, she reaches out to others in helping to meet their needs. She shows compassion and understanding to all, lending a helping hand to those in need.

31:21—*LAMED, LAMEDH*—'L'—staff; control; prod; urge forward; press on: "*She is not afraid of snow for her household, for all her household is clothed with scarlet.*" This "virtuous wife" has confidence that her preparations will keep her household comfortable. "*Not afraid*" (Heb. *lo, loh, yare*—*lo-yaw-ray*—a negative fear which is made positive) is a phrase which means 'showing self-assurance' that any catastrophic event or 'tough times' can be met and overcome. *"Snow"* represents a problem or disaster for which she has prepared in advance to overcome. *"Scarlet"* is a warm and rich color and is symbolic not just to the clothing she makes, but to all her loving care. She is completely secure with her husband and household.

31:22—*MEM*— 'm'—water; chaos; massive; deep: *"She makes tapestry for herself; her clothing is fine linen and purple."* This is an interesting verse in that it not only shows that she makes fine clothing to enjoy for herself but because she wants to please her husband. The word for clothing (actually a double word) in Hebrew is most interesting: (Heb. *l'buwsh—l'-bush—leb-oosh*—a garment; by implication (euphemistically) a wife; clothed with.) It literally means that a wife dresses to make herself attractive to her husband! ('Euphemistically' is an adverb describing a mild or indirect expression of thought or action, showing here that she dresses with clothing that compliments her inner qualities and exhibits modestly.) She is always keeping her husband in mind in whatever she does. In doing so, she is honoring God, who joined them together; the wife being a "reflection" of the heart of her husband

31:23—*NUN*— 'n'—fish; to spout; heir; prominent: *"Her husband is known in the gates when he sits among the elders of the land."* Her husband can concentrate on his job or local governing affairs because everything at home is peaceful and orderly due to his wife. He has a prominent position in the area. (Heb. *yada—yaw-dah'*—known; skillful; teach; have understanding; solve; *yashab*—to sit as a judge; to settle something; compliment.) He has a reputation in the community of someone whom a person can go to for help or advice. (This doesn't mean that he necessarily has an official position or authority in the area; it is his character and abilities that attracts people to him.) The pronoun *"Her"* beginning this verse also reflects on the fact that she is a compliment to him.

31:24—*SAMEKH*—'c' or 's' 'x'—sharp—to support; seed; prop up; aid; assist: *"She makes linen garments and sells them, and supplies sashes for the merchants."* Here again, she is referred to as a businesswoman who makes fine clothes to sell, as well as belts or girdles for the merchants. She is quite a motivated and resourceful woman who not only manages a neat, clean, and orderly household for her husband but also runs two or three successful businesses that profit her family. Her businesses seem to at least be in agriculture (see verse 16) and clothing, and she apparently is a regular supplier to merchants in her business.

(Reference here *could*, but not necessarily, be a situation whereby the husband is not capable of working. He may be somewhat incapacitated, and she may have to support him; or help financially through her businesses.)

31:25—*AIN, AYIN*—'silent' or 'guttural h'—eye; look; appearance; to see: *"Strength and honor are her clothing; she shall rejoice in time to come."* She has dignity and deep-seated joy, a cheerful spirit with an optimistic outlook. (Heb. *'oz 'oz*—security; majesty; strength.) This has to do with **inward** strength of character, and her *"rejoicing"* (Heb. *-sahaq—saw-hak*—laugh; make merry) shows her confident and bright spirit—she is continually and joyfully optimistic for the future. Her soul is prepared for whatever comes in that she trusts God completely. She's content in the relationship with her husband, her 'special man.' (This refers back to verses 21 and 22; she is inwardly relaxed in both soul and body, reflecting the love of her husband.)

31:26—*PE, PHE, PEY*—'p' or 'f'—word; mouth; speak; open; a beginning: *"She opens her mouth with wisdom, and on her tongue is the law of kindness."* When speaking, she does so wisely and in an encouraging manner (Heb. *chesed—kheh-sed*—kindly; lovingly; piety; -toward God-; grace.) She lifts up others. She does not gossip, talk down to people, or denigrate her husband. Having the *law of kindness* reveals her 'modus operandi'—that is, she speaks through her inner Godly character, principles of God (Heb. *torah*—the Pentateuch; law-of God) with kindness and grace. (She follows Isaiah 40:1: *"Comfort, O comfort my people, says your God."*) She may also be involved with some teaching of children and counseling other women in the neighborhood.

31:27—*TZADDI, TSADHE, TSADE*—*'s'* 'ts'—need; desire; to pull toward; destination; a harvest rake: *"She watches over the ways of her household, and does not eat the bread of idleness."* She is continually alert and involved in the ongoing procedures of her household. And even though she may take a restful repose at times, she is not lazy. She makes sure things are done right and properly.

31:28—*KOPH, QOPH, QOF*—'q' or 'k'—what is behind; back of; final: *"Her children_rise up and call her blessed; her husband also, and he praises her."* As her children consider

(Heb. *qum—koom*—confirm; uphold; rise) what she does and continues to do, they praise her. Learning from her valuable instruction and principles brings understanding that they can have success in life as they review their childhood and act upon the guidance and teaching that she has brought into their lives. *"Her husband also..."* reflects back and *"praises her."*

He is thankful for not only what she does in helping him raise their children and keeping the household in excellent shape, but also for what she has meant to him. She is a very real part of his happiness and success in life.

31:29—RESH—'r'—person; a head; what is the highest; most important; chief: *"Many daughters have done well, but you excel them all."* Here she's compared to several women in the community who also have very good reputations as wives and mothers, but she *"excels"* them all. (Heb. *alah -aw-law*—high; ascend; excel.) The comparison is done mostly by her children and her husband (ref. verse 28), but no doubt by others as well.

31:30—*SCHIN, SHIN*—'s' or 'sh'—eat; consume; devour; sharp; El Shaddai (God): *"Charm is deceitful, and beauty is passing, but a woman who fears the Lord, she shall be praised."*

A woman can possess beauty and graciousness (Heb. *chen*—*khane*—kindness; precious; grace; charm) and find favor among people, but this can be thought "vanity"—physical beauty eventually fades away. What really matters is reverencing (Heb. *yare*—*yaw-ray*—reverent; fear) God and living a Godly life. (Solomon agrees—*Song of Solomon 12:13*.) Here the virtuous woman is known by her reverential devotion to God. The Word of God is in her soul and is recognized by her husband as such through his soul relationship with her—again, they are true "soulmates."

31:31—*TAU, TAV*—'t' or 'th'—a mark; sign; ownership; signal; join together; a mark of strength; covenant; the last: *"Give her of the fruit of her hands, and let her own works praise her in the gates."* From the products of her hands—be it at home or in the community—her works show forth her worthiness. In this, she is a testimony of spiritual and physical love, both in the home and in public. Her own works bring her dignity—she is not trying to prove anything; this is just what she is. She has been nurtured by God into exemplifying the prototype of a Godly, virtuous woman concentrating on her special man through her soul love for him. This spreads out not only into her household but to her community as well, thereby causing high praise from others.

+++

The following list summarizes the characteristics of the *Proverbs 31* woman:

1. She is a rare woman (*"Who can find a virtuous wife?"* vs. 10).

2. She is capable and trustworthy.

3. She reflects the heart of her trusting husband.

4. She is a good worker and wise shopper for her household.

5. She is an excellent manager of her household and business ventures.

6. She has strength of character and singleness of purpose.

7. She is a benefit and help to others.

8. She is secure, confident, and excels in what she does.

9. She is supportive to her husband and honors him and God.

10. She is alert to the needs of her husband and household.

11. She is motivated and resourceful.

12. She has dignity and is cheerfully optimistic.

13. She is highly praised by her children, husband, and the community.

14. She has deep reverence for God.

But what about physical beauty? Is the concept of a virtuous woman as given here in these verses dismiss or demean beauty?

Not in the least! Beauty is from God and is everywhere—in nature, in all His creation—and in mankind. Beauty, true, is best evidenced among humans in character, sacrifice, love, and devotion. No matter what a person's physical appearance, God relishes in an honest and true worship of Him. Character is of most importance. A person can be physically unattractive but beautiful in character, or physically beautiful but unattractive in character. A beautiful character can often cause a physically unattractive person to **look** more attractive, and vice-versa. Note that the virtuous woman in *Proverbs 31* is defined through her beautiful and stable character, and not through any positive physical appearance she might possess. Physical beauty concerning an ideal virtuous woman may not be mentioned here, but it is throughout the Bible to show that this also is something to appreciate and enjoy. The following scriptures reveal that physical beauty if a woman happens to have it, is a desirable and positive attribute, but it does not in any way surpass beauty of character and soul: *Genesis 29:17; 2 Samuel 11:2; Esther 2:7; Songs 6:4.*

HOWEVER... let us also consider that in the last analysis, as the saying goes, "Beauty is in the eye of the beholder." It behooves the beholder, then, to determine where the true beauty lies—and hopefully, the beholder will probe the inner character traits to discover the 'truth' of a person.

FIVE

The Concept of 'Special' Man & 'Special' Woman

When God created the man, Adam He also included the woman, later to be named Eve, and built (fashioned) Eve from him and brought her to him. The Hebrew word for create is *bara*, which means to 'bring into existence,' the word used when God develops mankind into reality. In *Genesis 1:27,* when God creates man, the Word reads "*in the image of God He created **him**,*" which is a singular personal pronoun phrase. In the same sentence, it is further explained that He created **both**; "*male and female created He **them***" (emphasis mine), which is a plural pronoun phrase. This shows that the souls, or personalities, were created at the same time and placed into <u>one</u> body. After creating the animals and Adam naming them, God then proceeds to *make* (Heb. *banah*, to fashion; build; to make from material) a body for the woman from **material** taken **from man**. The word *bara* refers to the total creation of man and woman with the placing of both entities into a single body God had formed for them. Later God separated the female from the male and fashioned another physical body for her—(*banah*)—after He had placed the man in the Garden, who then named the animals. Adam, in *Genesis* 2:23, calls her "*wo-man because she was taken **out of man**.*" (Emphasis mine.) In other words, she *existed inside* the body of the man—being *created* along with the man—**before** she was *taken out* of the body of man. Adam responds with joy when he sees the woman,—the word "*said*" (Heb. *'amar*=call out; boast) refers, in context with "*this is*"(Heb. *'zoth'*), which is a highly excited astonishment in exclamatory speech. Adam makes his claim to her as being especially made for him in that she was **made from his body**—this is **his** bone and flesh. There was no other living creature that was found a *"help meet* (suitable) *for him"* (Gen.*2:20*–Heb. *'neged'*= counterpart, mate; a *special* fit). Nor did God build two or three or more women for Adam to choose. Just one—and she is his uniquely—physiologically, psychologically, mentally, and spiritually. Eve was Adam's "soulmate" in every way. She was his "special woman," designed by God for the man. And by the same token, he was her "special man."

Whereas God takes the woman *out* of man, He brings her *back* unto the man to be joined with him in one flesh again—but in a very different way (*Genesis 1:24*).

In our society concerning mates, we hear such comments as "...looking for that *special* one"; "...haven't met the *right one* yet"; "...we have so much *in common*"; "...we are *soulmates*". Then the question—"Are marriages made in heaven"? It appears, at least, that many sense there may very well be a 'special person' out there to discover for a lifetime spouse. So the question rounds out to: "Is there actually a *particular special* woman for a man, and a *particular special* man for a woman?" It is understood that it certainly was for Adam and Eve. God has placed a very high order on marriage. It is the basic foundation for all that follows in the setting up of society and government and is given for **all** mankind to enjoy (cf. *Ecclesiastes 9:9*).

One of the attributes of God is that He is very detailed about things, being very *precise* about the Law, rules, and worship services, as well as precise in choosing particular people to be rulers such as Moses and Aaron, and the kings and the prophets. In calling out the prophets, he chooses men who have an affinity for their special ministry and certain personality traits as a testimony to the people. For example, Jeremiah, who was a sweet and mild-mannered person and often called "the weeping prophet," is given one of the toughest and hardest messages of all the prophets to preach to his people—who, by the way, he dearly loves. His impassioned pleas to his people reveal God's deep love and concern for them, and the warning of severe judgment and exile if they did not repent is given deeper meaning and intensity through Jeremiah's personality traits and character, which is probably the—or a—reason God chose him.

God was also very precise, as seen in *Genesis 24,* concerning the search to find a wife for Isaac. A careful reading of this lengthy chapter of 27 verses will reveal the specific intricate details to be followed in the choice of a *special* woman for Isaac. These intimate details certainly show God's directive guidance in the choosing of the *specific* and *right* woman for Isaac. The **Book of Ruth,** concerning Ruth and Boaz, can also give understanding to the concept of 'special man' and 'special woman' being brought together by God, as will be discussed later.

Many times, if not always, people with certain personality and attitudes needed for a specific calling are chosen for the particular tasks God has for them. This is seen all through scripture and also evidenced today as certain people are "called" for specific ministries. This is also true concerning marriage—a special specific woman for a specific man, and vice versa.

As related earlier, marriages between men and women and the establishment of families are a most important foundation for the establishment of an orderly society. A marriage must be firmly rooted in areas such as morality, honesty, and of course, real love. That is why it is so important for a marriage to be made up of a man and a woman who are *right* for each other—in other words, *special* for each other. Henceforth the following will be used in this thesis for "special woman" and "special man": i.e., SW for special woman and SM for special man.

An important verse in the study of SW and SM is from Solomon in *Ecclesiastes 9:9*: *"Live joyfully with **the wife** whom you love all the days of your vain life **which He has given you** under the sun, all your days of vanity, for that is your portion (reward) in life, and in the labor which you perform under the sun."* (Emphasis mine.) A prominent phrase in this verse is *"which He has given you."* The word *"given"* here in Hebrew is *nathan* (naw-than'), a primitive root meaning, in the context of the subject of this verse, 'the **wife'**—who is placed into her role as wife *(given)* by appointment, or assignment. The pronoun "He" refers to God, who is the One who gives (prescribes) the wife to the man. In His giving or gifting, God is matching the appointed or prescribed woman (SW) that He assigned to the man (SM) in marriage. This verse indicates that the best "reward" that a man can achieve in life *is* his wife—the good and right SW as a wife especially designed for him.

Proverbs 18: 22 further states that the Lord is pleased when a man *"finds"* a wife: *"He who finds a wife finds a good thing, and obtains favor from the Lord."* The word for *"favor"* in Hebrew is *"ratson,"* a strong masculine noun, meaning *delight* and *goodwill* **from a superior to an inferior** who has willingly obeyed a directive or an instruction.

In context, the Lord takes pleasure and is favorably disposed toward the man who seeks and finds the SW that God has designed and planned for him.[1] The concept of *ratson* is reinforced in *Proverbs 19:14*: *"Houses and riches are an inheritance from*

---

1 It is interesting to note that the Septuagint (LXX)—the Old Testament in Greek—adds a two-statement dispatch note to *Proverbs 18:22*, where the first statement says: *"He that puts away a good wife puts away a good thing (happiness)…",* the idea here that having a good wife is the basic foundation upon which true and lasting happiness is built. (Solomon evidently did not find true happiness in a wife as revealed in his writings, especially *Ecclesiastes* and *Song*s.)

fathers, ***but a prudent wife is from the Lord.*** *"* (Emphasis mine.*)* Only the Lord can provide a prudent wife, and He has set this up universally for all mankind, which is more important than obtaining *"houses and riches."*

And if the Lord is the One who is providing the wife and working to bring SW to SM, it behooves the man in his searching to find a wife (and the woman as well concerning a husband) to pray and seek the Lord's leading in this. She is a ***special*** (and prominent) ***gift*** the man receives from the Lord. And the believer who fully trusts the Lord to find his SW will succeed. (In reference back to *Ecclesiastes 9:9,* we see again that the Lord's gift of 'special man' (SM) 'special woman' (SW) is given to **all,** believer and unbeliever. As previously noted, it is God's gift to all mankind. A believer having received the Lord Jesus Christ as personal savior who is searching for his/her special mate via **God's will and principles** will almost certainly find that person. (The unbeliever can also find the right mate, albeit through possibly more difficulties.) And so the first marriage was performed by God Himself. He brought the bride "down the aisle," so to speak, to the groom (*Genesis 2:22*)—and joined them together, a covenant relationship which is next explored.

SIX

The Marriage Covenant

Marriage is indeed a special covenant between man and woman and must be taken seriously. The misuse and breaking of the marriage covenant is an illustration given in the book of *Malachi* in which the prophet shows the seriousness of not only this but of all covenants, and especially the covenant between the Lord and His people. When the people act wickedly and cry out to God because of the hurt and suffering caused by their sin, the Lord reveals their sin of breaking a marriage covenant with each other as a serious prime example of the nation breaking its covenant with Him: *"And this is the second thing you do: You cover the altar of the Lord with tears, with weeping and crying; so He does not regard the offering anymore, nor receive it with goodwill from your hands. Yet you say, "For what reason?" Because the Lord has been witness between you and the **wife of your youth**, with whom you have dealt treacherously, yet she is your companion and **your wife by covenant**. But did He not make them one, having a remnant of the Spirit? And why one? He seeks godly offspring, therefore take heed to your spirit, and let none deal treacherously with **the wife of his youth**."* (*Malachi 2:13-15*; emphasis mine). The Jews have a history of looking upon marriage as being a very sacred covenant between each other and with God. They understand that the marriage covenant is as important as any other covenant where God is also a part. In using marriage, as an illustration, Malachi is teaching people the seriousness of their unfaithfulness towards God, which is likened unto something they may clearly

40

understand —the treacherously serious sin of their unfaithfulness to each other in marriage.

The phrase *"wife of your (his) youth"* repeated twice in these verses along with *"your wife by covenant"* illustrates the importance of the marriage covenant. The phrase *"wife of your youth"* also occurs in *Proverbs 5:18*, wherein the previous verses of this chapter, the wife is compared to belonging to the husband as much as his private water well, or cistern, belongs to him. The wife is also compared to be like a loving deer and a graceful doe, satisfying the husband: *"Drink water from your own cistern and running water from your own well. Should your fountains be disbursed abroad, streams of water in the streets? Let them be only your own, and not for strangers with you. Let your fountain be blessed and rejoice with <u>the wife of your youth</u>. As a loving deer and a graceful doe, let her breasts satisfy you at all times; and always be enraptured with her love. For why should you, my son, be enraptured by an immoral woman, and be embraced in the arms of a seductress?" (Proverbs 5:15-20)*. The phrase *"wife of your youth"* as previously shown in other scriptures as well, was in the ancient Hebrew culture a complex phrase with serious and deep meaning. The words (more than one) for wife (Hebrew: *min, min-nay; ishshah, nashiym*) in parenthetical context means "a woman that is a part of (wife to) a union which began in youth"—the youth of both the man and the woman. The word for youth being a properly, or perfect, passive participle takes its meaning in this phrase from the word for 'wife,' and concerns a time and event being a singular one-time occurrence, which stands as a covenant indefinitely until fulfilled, or rather revoked as in death—the only way for the marriage to end. (This is much like a legal will.) And in these verses, the word for 'strange woman' or 'stranger' (Heb. *nokriy-nok-ree'—nok-ry-nok-re*) means an 'adulterous; a foreigner; an alien.' It is very apparent that all these verses concerning the relationships of men and women are very serious elements to be taken into thoughtful consideration before one is pledged to them.

We saw the development of Adam and Eve in the beginning of creation that God created two entities (souls/spirits, male and female) and placed them in one physical body. Then building another body, He separated the entities and placed one—the female—in that second body, and brought that body back to the first—now containing only one of the entities, the male, to begin a <u>different</u> union between the two bodies from which to start the family. When we start thinking about the marriage process, we need to start where God started—by matching the 'right' man and 'right' woman to be united in ***holy matrimony***, fitted for each other in all ways possible. This uniting or merging together is not just physically, but also mentally, emotionally, and spiritually to become one flesh. The evil barriers to this happening are an independent spirit, selfishness, and the lack of real love.

"Evil?" Yes—anything is evil when it disrupts God's plan and purpose for His created order.

God creates and builds the first two people and then turns the process of bringing other people into existence over to these two people—Adam and Eve. "*Marriage is honorable among all, and the bed* (of marriage) *undefiled, but fornicators and adulterers God will judge. (Hebrews, 13:4).* The Lord's purpose for His highest creation—man—is for a monogamous relationship between one man and one woman for the family to be established in which children are raised having a father and a mother. This is the central main purpose of God creating two sexes, one male and the other female. Any other type of sexual relationship—such as pre-marital, homosexual, or any other type—is sinful in that it is a *distortion* of God's creative order and purpose and is based upon selfish, independent carnal desires. These other types are definitely **evil** because they completely flaunt the Creator God. Marriage indeed is a very sacred and holy procedure and must be treated as such. Unfortunately, this is what so many fail to do—King Solomon as an example with his thousand wives and concubines, a subject which will continue to be discussed later in more detail. Even today, in our society, many marriage ceremonies include such phrases as "What God hath joined together, let no man put asunder." This indicates that many tend to believe (or acknowledge) that God is involved in their marriage (as He is with all His other covenants). And the foundation upon which marriage—in fact, all of God's covenants with His people—are built is **love.** And just what **is** love? Or rather—what **kind** of love are we speaking of? What now follows is an attempt to describe these various kinds of love before continuing with the subject of marriage.

(In searching the Word of God, we can obtain a clearer understanding of love. The Bible states that God is love (*1 John 4:8*), and it follows that all real or perfect love originates with God, who through His earthly personage had much to say about the subject.)

SEVEN

Defining the Types of Love

A family man arrives at his home after a long day's work. As he steps through the door, he is greeted by his wife and young children. Hugs and kisses are exchanged. His dog comes up to him, wagging her tail. He reaches down and greets the dog calling her name and rubs her head. He smells the air and is enticed by the fragrance of one of his special desserts. He exclaims, "Apple pie! I love apple pie"! He turns back to his wife, looks fondly at her, and says, "I love you, honey!" He pauses, and then bending down to his small children, a boy, and a girl, exclaims, "I love you both, my dear children!" He looks toward his dog standing by with tail still wagging and says," I love you too, Lassie"!

This man has just expressed three prominent types of love. The Greek language best explains these types of love. Before we go further into the discussion of marriage, there needs to be a basic understanding of these kinds of love. Even though there are up to seven words in the Greek defining a particular type of love, there are three basic words for love, which are the most common and best define the subject for our discussion. These three Greek words are *eros, phileo (fil-eh-o),* and *agape (*noun: *ag-ah'-pay';* verb form- *agapao: ag-ap-ah-o'). Eros* is a self-centered, selfish type of love; *phileo* is more of a brotherly or friendship type of love, and *agape* is other-centered, sacrificial, self-less love. *Eros* is a word hardly used in scripture at all (although the Hebrew word construction *ahab,* or *aheb-}aw-hab', aw-habe; agav*—can mean this in context, as when Isaac requested his son Esau to bring him his favorite meat and exclaimed—*"such as I love…that I may*

44

eat"(Genesis 27:1-4). This type of love is driven by lust—it is short-lived and fades away after being satisfied. (The English words 'erotic' and 'error' stem from *eros*.)

Phileo and *agape* are used many times in Scripture. In the example above, the family man coming home to his family and smelling the apple pie is exclaiming an *eros* type love, which is gratified only by eating the pie, which, of course, ends the existence of the pie. *Eros* love is selfish love seeking only to satisfy the self. In greeting and patting his dog, the man is showing *phileo* love, a 'friendship bond' with his dog. (The expression, "a dog is man's best friend," suffices here.) The American city Philadelphia is called the "city of brotherly love"; *phileo (love)* and *delphi* (city). As previously noted, this type of love is friendship or brotherly love and the like. *Agape* love is focused upon the 'other'—apart from self, even to the point of the one expressing this type of love being sacrificial for the benefit of another. It is the highest and greatest form of love. In the above illustration, the family man greeting his wife and children is expressing *agape* love. In this type of love, the man is willing to sacrifice himself in whole or part for the benefit of his family.

This is the kind of sacrificial love that Jesus calls us to, and further explains that this is the greatest type of love: *"This is my commandment, that you love (agapao[1]) one another as I have loved you. No one has greater love than this, that a man lay down his life for his friends." (John 15:12-13)*. Note that this love is *commanded* or required. This is also the type of love that Jesus calls a man to express in marriage to his wife:*" Husbands, love (agapao[1]) your wives, even as Christ also loved the church and gave Himself for it..." (Ephesians 5:25)*. And how did Christ love

---

1 As an active verb form, *agapao* indicates that it is a mental (cognitive) direction of the will. It is **not** emotion; rather, emotion brings color and appreciation to the cognitive, enhancing what the cognitive "discovers" or develops.

the church? He died for it. And this is what a husband is called to do for his wife if a situation necessitates it. To repeat: *agape* love is given by our Lord as a **command** to us (*John 15:12*).

How can one know which type of love he or she is most usually operating under? One possible clue might be in conversation with others. If one's main conversational theme is more about self than the other person, and rarely inquiring about the other person's status, interests, and history, then it would appear that that person is operating under eros love—love of self. Agape—and even phileo love—reveals genuine interest and concern of and for the other person.

As revealed in *1 Corinthians 13:13b*: "*...but the greatest of these is love* (agape)." Genuine love of the brethren, highlighted in many scriptural verses, is to be paramount in a Christian's life, and is even a 'test' of whether or not a person is really exhibiting a Christian lifestyle.

This is the type of love that a marriage should have in order for it to succeed; it is to think the **other** more important than the self.

These types of love are explained next in more detail, especially concerning marriage, as the discussion of this subject continues.

EIGHT

Marriage As It Should Be

Marriages fail because of one basic reason: **selfishness** *(eros).* Whether it be financial, sickness, or hardship of any kind, when *eros* is stronger than any other type of love, the marriage will fail, sooner or later. When two people decide to live together and not be married until they "discover" whether or not they are "compatible," that relationship is off on the wrong premise. Suppose a couple decides that going through a marriage ceremony is unnecessary and can just live and love together. In that case, the thought most probably exists in the back of their mind—(if they are painfully honest with themselves)—that they are not "hooked" and can get out of the situation and just escape, or walk away and become "free" again. They are forgetting—or never really learned—is that marriage is a whole-hearted commitment—with nothing held back and expressing real love; and necessary to legally protect family members concerning ownership, inheritance, and other areas of family life. But what should be considered to be even more important is the fact that marriage is God's basic creative and sacred foundation for mankind in procreation (family), society, and even governmental authority. It is a *sacred covenant* relationship between man and wife, and yes—God. (Refer again to the statement on *Malachi 2:13-15,* as explained in chapter six.) To ignore the marriage ceremony—which, like other covenants, is an oral and mental sacred pledge—is to trample on God's design for mankind in the creation of the man and the woman. It was God, after all, who created marriage and everything that goes with it. At the end of many wedding ceremonies is the statement referred to earlier that is common: "What God has joined together, let not man put asunder." However, marriage is not just two people falling in love, getting married, and living happily ever after. The "living happily ever after" is the hard part. It is work. And as previously mentioned, not everyone is automatically guaranteed to find the best or highest form of love. It is anomalous to believe that anyone can just "fall in (the right kind of) love." Every human being experiences love—the *eros* kind, that is. As young children mature, they soon learn and experience the next higher love, *phileo* —friendships are formed, and most everyone usually does give forth this type of love.

The highest form of love—*agape* (selfless; sacrificial) is not achieved by everyone. It is paramount to have this type of love in order for a marriage to survive "until death do us part." It has to be experienced and even taught in a person's upbringing. A person must be cognitively and emotionally mature enough for it to be a stable part of his or her character. And even though a child may have this capacity to least some extent early on (yes, even a child can exhibit sacrificial love), society does not allow marriages between children because of not only physical but also mental and emotional immaturity. Love is not just emotion—it is, first and foremost, a *cognitive mental attitude*. Because it is cognitive, it can be **commanded**—which is what Jesus stated, as explained earlier. Emotions have no cognition—they are **responders** to what cognition teaches them. Emotions are unstable and must be directed by proper mental attitude if they are to do what they are designed to do—bring appreciation and "color" to what the mind has discovered and takes in. When the emotions are not controlled by the mind (cognition), chaos results. They can actually take control of the cognitive and produce negative results, such as hate, wrongful biases, irrational decisions, and the like. And in human relationships, this spells disaster. *Eros* (selfish) love originates and works mostly from the emotions and is a very powerful—and many times destructive—force in human nature.

Many marriages are based on an *eros* type of love on the part of one or both of the mates. These marriages cannot succeed on eros alone even though some of them may last for years, but sooner or later can decay and even turn into hatred as the self is "compressed" by the other. Such selfish love in the extreme is continually focused on take, take, and continual taking to gratify self. Even if there is any giving by the self, it is often only to obtain satisfaction of the self in return.

A marriage and other relationships which are based on *phileo* love (friendship) can last for a long time—even perhaps indefinitely. There is a give and take here, a balancing in which the self takes and gives, resulting in a more stable relationship. In this type of relationship, satisfaction is achieved in the giving as well as in the taking. There must be a balance in this, for in the taking—and even in the giving—there could be a strain on the relationship which could cause it to end. Lasting friendship involves both parties genuinely giving and receiving. That being said, however, there is another factor in this type of friendship love, which can grow into something else. That something, of course, is *agape* love, which as noted in the last chapter, as defined by Jesus; and being of such importance, He began this discourse with the disciples by stating that it is now a new commandment: *"A new commandment I give to you, that you love one another; as I have loved you, that you also love one another." (John 13:34)* It is a command to the cognitive, not to emotion. *Agape* love is, as mentioned above, a **mental** attitude, not an emotional response. *Eros* love, being addictively emotive and selfish, usually cannot last or morph into other types of love and almost always ends in destructive relationships. The other types of love are lasting and can merge together, such as in a marriage where husband and wife are best of friends as well as lovers. For *eros* to remain, it needs these other kinds of love to continue existing. Attractions to the opposite sex often start as an *eros* love, and as the relationship deepens, then *phileo* and *agape* loves can come into the picture. And here is where *agape* and *eros* can fortify each other and deepen the relationship. This not only allows *eros* love to survive but also the other love types can continue to grow and deepen as long as *eros* (if it is involved) is "controlled" by a higher love, such as *agape*—or even *phileo*. In fact, *eros* love **needs** a higher love in order to be sustainable. Unfortunately, however, selfish *eros* love is so prevalent that the other love-types are made more difficult to achieve, especially *agape* love. *Agape* love is much more of a rarity, and as mentioned earlier, it seems that many do not or are unable to achieve it.

This was the case with Peter when, after the resurrection, Jesus asked him if he loved Him. Jesus posed the question to Peter three times. Peter responded every time with *phileo* type love, failing to commit himself to loving Jesus with *agape* love, most probably under the embarrassment of having denied knowing Jesus three times (*Matthew 26:69-75*). Upon asking the question again the third time, Jesus, having twice asked for *agape* love, addressed Peter at his level and posed the third question with *phileo* love, to which Peter responded that this was what he was trying to tell the Lord. Peter, no doubt greatly shaken in his denial of Jesus, felt he could not come up to the high standards to which Jesus was calling him. The Lord accepted this from Peter, knowing he would prove the kind of love Jesus wanted by the sacrifice of his own life later in his testimony to the Lord.[1]

When the apostle Paul in *Ephesians 5* speaks about a man loving his wife to the point of self-sacrifice, he is speaking of *agape* love. This love was expressed by God for mankind, as exemplified by the Messiah Jesus Christ on the cross. *Agape* love brings the highest fulfillment and satisfaction that can be had in this life for those who are willing to sacrificially develop such love. This is the kind of love, toward God (and toward mankind implied), which Solomon wisely stated in the ending of his 'confessional,' that is the only **real** purpose in life: *"Let us hear the conclusion of the matter: fear God and keep His commandments, For this is man's all." (Ecclesiastes 12:13)*. As previously explained, not everybody attains this, but it is worth the effort and reward, sometimes no matter what the cost to finally achieve it.

And even the most wicked sinner on his deathbed, having failed to find or develop satisfying love in his lifetime, can achieve it from our Lord as did the thief on the cross in the last few minutes of his life when he turned to Christ on His cross and asked for remembrance, to which Jesus said: *"Today you shall be with me in Paradise" (Luke 23:39-43)*. We can see examples in human

---

1 Jesus knew that Peter was focused completely on Him and His ministry and was very enthusiastic in following Him. Peter twice jumped out of a boat to be with Jesus—("*And Peter answered him and said, 'Lord if it is You, command me to come to You on the water.' So He said, "Come." And when Peter had come down out of the boat, he walked on the water to go to Jesus." Matthew 14:28-29,* and *"Therefore, that disciple whom Jesus loved said to Peter, "It is the Lord!" Now when Simon Peter heard that it was the Lord, he put on his outer garment for he had removed it, and plunged into the sea" John 21:7)*. The gospels also give account of Peter following the soldiers that arrested Jesus in the garden (*Matthew 26:58*) and also the fact that Peter cut off the high priest's servant's ear (*John 18:10*)—he was ready and willing to fight for his Lord and Master no matter what. These are hardly the actions of a person who is not so completely dedicated to a person or cause that he would fight and die for his commitment. Peter was completely immersed in Jesus. Peter's denial of Christ was totally due to the **momentary** (emphasis mine) weakness of his abject fear in the situation, and not in any way to a traitorous mind-set, as in the case of Judas, the betrayer of our Lord Jesus Christ.

life of this kind of love's potency in a situation where a person sacrifices his life for that of another—or when one loses a beloved spouse through death. When this loss happens in a marriage, the one flesh concept is broken up or separated. The "oneness" of the two becomes single again, bringing the despair of loneliness— often something that is very difficult to bear. The gospel of the Christian faith, with the promise of the Resurrection to life eternal and permitting the entry into Heaven for all who believe and accept Jesus Christ as their personal savior, brings an ending to the severe aspects of despair and loneliness. All Heaven is cradled in the perfect redeeming *agape* love of God where the saints—' true believers'—are reunited with saved loved ones in blissful everlasting life.

What happens, however, according to Biblical teaching, when a marriage does end due to the death of one of the spouses? When death takes one, the other is free to remarry, as the Law in God's Word explains:" *For the married woman was bound by law to the living husband. But if the husband is dead, she is set free from the law of her husband. So then, while her husband lives, she is married to another man, she shall be called an adulteress. But if the husband dies, she is free from the law, she is no adulteress by becoming another man's wife"* (*Romans 7:2-3*). And again: "*A wife is bound by law as long as her husband lives; but if her husband dies, she is at liberty to be married to whom she wishes, only in the Lord.*"(*1 Corinthians 7:39*).

These verses indicate that a marriage relationship between a man and woman is for this life only. (See *Matthew 22:30* for Jesus' teaching on this.) But then there is something else here in the last phrase of the scripture just quoted, which was discussed earlier concerning SW and SM. The wife, being free to marry whomsoever she will if her husband dies, is to do this "*only in the Lord.*" Of course, this means being a Christian, and she must marry a Christian; however, this phrase means more than that. "*in the Lord*" means in the **will** of the Lord. She must seek out a man that the Lord chooses for her new husband. (The man must also be doing the same.) She should seek the Lord's guidance in this important matter and marry the believer that the Lord has for her—the sacred union of SW with SM—if she seeks remarriage. (And whereas full happiness and satisfaction in life is God's gift for *all* humanity, those who are not Christian can and should find the right mate for life's greatest reward and happiness. It is just deeper, better, and easier for believers.)

This was the situation between Ruth and Boaz, as seen in the biblical book of **Ruth**. Naomi was an Israelite woman who, with her husband, moved to the land of Moab, where her sons met and married Moabite women—one whose name was Ruth. They lived there for at least ten years, during which time Naomi's husband and her two sons died. Being now alone, Naomi decided to move back to Israel, and one of her daughters-in-law, Ruth, decided to go back with her. Ruth made a full and genuine commitment to live with her mother-in-law and accept her people and her God. And so the two widows made their journey to Israel.

Shortly after their arrival into Naomi's hometown Ruth meets Boaz. They marry when Boaz discovers there is no closer 'kinsman-redeemer'—a relative according to the Law to carry on the family's name—to prevent him from marrying Ruth. This wonderful love story is detailed in the four chapters of the biblical book of **Ruth**, and both are listed as being in the messianic genealogy of our Lord and Savior Jesus Christ (*Matthew 1:5*).

It can be said with certainty that Ruth and Boaz were 'right' for each other—SW with SM—as God certainly engineered their coming together in marriage. But can it be said that Ruth's first husband was her SM for their approximately ten years of marriage? Or that Boaz, the second husband, was her real SM? From all that is taught in the Law, and what has been reviewed here on the subject concerning God's "programming" or designing, the right man for the right woman and vice versa, it would certainly indicate that a person can have more than one spouse who is the right or "special one" as enabled especially by death, with God doing a "**reprograming**." If this is the case, then both men were the SM for Ruth.

And what about someone wanting to walk away from a marriage relationship or a man wanting to put away his wife because of infidelity, such as fornication? The Mosaic law does allow for a bill of divorcement. As Jesus Christ taught when asked why Moses authorized divorce: *"He said to them, 'Because of your hard-heartedness Moses allowed you to put away your wives; but from the beginning, it was not so."* (*Matthew 19:8*). And previous to saying this, Jesus had stated that *"what God has joined together let not man separate"* (*put asunder*-verse 6), thus reviewing again the importance of holding fast this sacred covenant of marriage. As reflected in the phrase *"from the beginning it was not so,"* it specifies God's will that the marriage relationship endure and not be broken up in any human way. But when someone just wants to walk away from a marriage—what then? Admittedly not an easy question to answer, but the question could be asked—"Was it *really* a marriage to begin with?" There might have been infidelity on the part of at least one, or they could have been simply unequally yoked. Whatever the situation, **sin** was certainly the basic cause of the separation. The confession and repentance of such a disunion and the asking of forgiveness should be made to the Lord in order to spiritually free a person.

Marriage, constructed by God and, when performed as it was made to be, is God's greatest gift to mankind apart from salvation. It should be treated with the utmost respect for the sacred covenant that it is.[2]

---

2 What is meant by marriage is the coupling of a man and a woman. Homosexual unions are not marriages and are condemned by God as an abomination: "*You shall not lie with mankind as with womankind. It is abomination to God*" (Leviticus *18:22*). "*If a man also lies with mankind, as he lies with a woman, both of them have committed an abomination. They shall surely be put to death. Their blood shall be upon them*"(*Leviticus 20:13*; cf. *Romans 1:26-27*). Sodom and Gomorrah were destroyed because of their extreme wickedness, homosexuality being their greatest sin (*Genesis 18:20; 19:4-5*). God loves the sinner, no matter how deep their wickedness, but hates their sin, and this can result in destructive consequences as with the twin cities of Sodom and Gomorrah.

NINE

Solomon's Love Life

Being the wisest man the world has ever known, save for Jesus Christ, our Lord, it behooves us to see what Solomon, under the guidance of the Holy Spirit, confirms in scripture concerning love and marriage. In his writing of *Proverbs,* Solomon gives much attention to the subject of immorality and warns of getting involved with the "strange women," meaning adulterous women. Chapter 5 of *Proverbs,* which was cited in an earlier chapter, is a good example of his giving this advice to his son concerning the subject. (This may have been what David counseled his son and also what Solomon himself learned. He is earnestly passing this advice onto his son and young men in general.) Other verses previously cited concerning Solomon's teaching on love and marriage (*Proverbs 18:22; 19:14; Ecclesiastes 9:9*)[1] reveal important insights on what God wants us to know about these matters. Utilizing his God-given wisdom, Solomon applies the subject to his own life as a testimony of warning to his son: "*I have not obeyed the voice of my teachers, nor inclined my ear to those who instructed me! I*

---

1 Solomon's book of *Proverbs* has much to say on the subject of this study concerning character, lifestyle, and loves; however, a detailed commentary on *Proverbs* would be a large enough volume in itself. *Ecclesiastes* would also be a like commentary but involving itself almost wholeheartedly on other subjects that exemplify the "vanity of life." This study gleans out only a very few verses in *Proverbs*—and to a lesser extent, *Ecclesiastes*—that pertain to women and marriage, which lend with other scriptures revealing Solomon's sinful womanizing lifestyle bringing him frustration, depression, and alienation from God. *Ecclesiastes* is Solomon's "confessional" in that he found just about everything in life to be "*vanity*"—not worth much of anything, especially if that life is devoid of God. The word "*vanity*" occurs 38 times in this book, and the phrase "*under the sun*" 29 times, meaning that if one's thoughts and motives are for this life only and not centered on God, then life indeed is—**"vanity."**

was on the verge of total ruin, in the midst of the assembly and congregation" (Proverbs 5:13-14). 'Don't think and do what I did,' he is trying to teach his son and other youths (cf. *Proverbs 1:4 & 4:1-2*).

What happened to Solomon is understandable, as no doubt, having a thousand women at his personal command brought many difficult complications and problems into his personal life as well as his kingship. Just to keep track of them and even remember all their names would seem to be an insurmountable task. Most, if not all of these women were united to Solomon in a **political contract,** as seen with his marriage to Pharaoh's daughter *(1 Kings 3:1)*, which was probably his first and more personal marriage relationship, in that soon after their union Solomon took her home with him. (It is interesting and significant to note that even though Solomon had hundreds of wives and concubines, so far as it is known, he only had one son and two daughters.)

He authored *Proverbs* (and copied some of them from his father David and other sources) later in life along with *Ecclesiastes* and "*The Song Of Solomon,*" the latter given in this study as a verse -by-verse commentary in the next section. It is in *Ecclesiastes,*[2] however, that an important confessional statement is recorded (and also echoed in *Proverbs 5:13-14* as just previously cited):'" *Here is what I have found,' says the Preacher, 'Adding one thing to the other to find out the reason, which **my soul still seeks** but I cannot find: One man among thousand I have found, but a woman among all of these **I have not found'**" (Ecclesiastes 7:27-28*—emphasis mine). Solomon is confessing here that even though he has found at least one man in a thousand that is a good or his best friend, in

---

2 *Ecclesiastes is* Greek for the Hebrew feminine participle **qoheleth** *(ko-hel-eth)* -'preacher', one who calls an assembly of people together for instruction. Hebrews often used feminine words to define groups and principles, as we do for ships.

spite of having access to his thousand women, he never found his true soulmate. (Concerning all the other women in his life, as was previously cited in chapter two, the statement of *1 Kings 11:2*, *"Solomon clung to these (women) in love,"* the word **clung** (Heb. *dabaq*=pursue hard; hold fast.)

In his God-given wisdom, he knows and has stated that the highest reward in life is the obtaining of a loving and prudent 'soulmate' wife in a genuine love/marriage situation. In his statement that he has not found a woman, he is saying that he has not discovered the 'special one' (SW) to be a loving wife to him.

It wasn't that he was not searching for her, for as he *"clung"* to all these women, he was very much involved in a rather desperate searching mode. At the end of his confessional of *Ecclesiastes*, however, he is saying that the best when all is said and done is an obedient relationship to God:" *Let us hear the conclusion of this whole matter: fear God and keep his commandments, for this is man's all"* (*Ecclesiastes 12:13*).

It seems very clear, then, that Solomon never found his SW. His statements in *Proverbs* and *Ecclesiastes*, as previously cited, certainly relate to this fact. He is led by the Holy Spirit in his writings to express his failures and shortcomings in order that his experiences in these areas might hopefully benefit not only his progeny but also all men (and yes, all persons) everywhere. He often warns, especially through his *Proverbs*, the serious effect of immorality on a person's life concerning men with women. This brought God's punishment upon him personally in the losing of his kingdom for his son, and eventually dividing the nation as well: *"So the Lord became angry with Solomon because his heart turned from the Lord God of Israel, who had appeared to him twice, and had commanded him concerning this thing, that he should not go after other gods; but he did not keep what the Lord had commanded. Therefore the Lord said to Solomon, "Because you have done this, and have not kept my covenant and my statutes, which I have commanded you, I will surely tear the kingdom away from you and give it to your servant. Nevertheless I will not do it in your days, for the sake of your father David; I will tear it out of the hand of your son." (1 Kings 11:9-12.)* His kingdom was split into two nations after his death.

In his third book of scriptural writings, Solomon details his attempt to court a beautiful young woman, whom he very well may have thought that she was the SW for him. This book, "*The Song of Solomon,*" is studied next in a verse-by-verse commentary.

TEN

THE SONG OF SOLOMON
A Commentary

The Biblical book '*Song of Solomon*' is quite a different thesis from most other books that make up the Holy Bible. (Martin Luther, who started the Protestant Reformation, wondered if this book should even be in the canon of scripture.) Known as the "*Song of Songs*" in Hebrew and "*Canticles*" (meaning "*Songs*" in Latin—the abbreviation sometimes used here), this is a fascinating and enigmatic book. It is unlike the other Solomonic literature of *Ecclesiastes* and *Proverbs,* which provide striking testimonials reflecting on the wide-ranging and unique wisdom of Solomon. It is designed in a poetic theatrical mode but too short for a theatrical presentation. He is noted for his writing of thousands of proverbs and over one thousand songs (*1 Kings 4:32*), but this is a very special one of his songs. Here, in even more detail than he expressed in his 'confessional' of *Ecclesiastes*, he humbly reviews his failure to court and win what he might have considered to be his SW, which he failed to find in the many hundreds of other women in his life.

There are various interpretations on just how to approach "*The Song of Solomon.*"

Four prominent ones are:

1. *Natural or liberal view*: "*Songs*" is simply a picture of human love, showing the highest form. This poetic writing gives forth a firm decree against an unbiblical dualism that holds the physical and material to be of lower estate than the spiritual—

that the unmarried state is more virtuous than that of matrimony. The poem elevates true human love as being a great blessing—perhaps the greatest blessing—from God. (As Solomon would agree, pertaining to his statement in *Ecclesiastes 9:9*.) And as the apostle Paul uses marriage in *Ephesians 4:25-28* to illustrate the nature of love between husband and wife and contrasts it with the relationship of Christ and His church, so *"Songs"* illustrates a pure and high commitment of chastity and love in marriage between man and woman, which can also be analogous to Christ and His church. So it is at least that.

2. *Allegorical:* Common among ancient Jews and later into the Christian church is the concept that *"Songs"* also expresses by this love story God's love to his chosen people in Hebrew (and Christian) worship and in relationship between Christ And the church. The main characters are Solomon (as God) and the Schulamite girl (as the believer); the character of the shepherd incidental. Most verses are able to be analogous to the Jewish and Christian faith.

3. *The Typical view:* The concept here is that "*Songs*" portrays the pure love between Christ and the Church, with King Solomon representing Christ, and the Shulamite girl the church, or the Christian. It does not seek special meaning for each verse, as the allegorical view often does. It also does not give much meaning, if any, to the third character, the shepherd.

4. *The Dramatic view*: Advocated by Franz Delitzsch (who, along with Carl F. Keil in 1864, published the famed 10 volume classic commentary on the Old Testament) once stated that "The 'Song' is the most obscure book in the Old Testament." This view holds that *"Songs"* is presented as a drama representing Solomon falling in love with a native girl and taking her into his harem to win her favors. It introduces the ***shepherd hypotheses****,* with the "shepherd lover" to whom the Shulamite girl remains faithful in spite of Solomon's advances. An extension of this view holds that Solomon represents the 'world'; the Shulamite girl as the believer of God (the 'chosen people'; the Church, or Christian), and her "shepherd lover"—who is *away for a time*—as God (Christ). It is this view which best fits the teachings of Scripture and with other aspects of Solomonic literature. In the enigmatic translation of the difficult Hebrew of "*Songs,*" the language, cultural phrases, and idioms strongly suggest this view. In the commentary which follows, precise translation of word and cultural structure from the Hebrew has shown this interpretation to be the most accurate and makes the most sense. (For clarity and smoothness of flow, these Hebrew words and phrases shown are limited.) Also, when viewed together with his other writings, a clearer picture of the man Solomon is revealed concerning his life and especially his loves. As previously noted, "*The Song of Solomon*" is unique because it is written like theatrical play, with the different characters speaking (or singing) as the story develops. In addition to Solomon, the Shulamite girl, and the shepherd lover, other characters are the 'daughters of Jerusalem' (Solomon's harem) and the brothers of the Shulamite girl. This Dramatic View is what the author holds to and interprets concerning *"Songs"*.

Song of Solomon Commentary: 1:1-17

1:1—Strongly stated, this opening sentence claims Solomon as the author. There is no reason for any other authorship; some have previously thought that the Shulamite girl might have been the author as she is the most prominent speaker, but there is nothing to back this up.

1:2—The Shulamite girl is longing for the kisses of her shepherd lover, even though she is in Solomon's harem. (Later, *"Songs"* explains how she got there.) This is a rather dramatic verse (no doubt never used as a "memory verse") depicting right away that this book may contain amorous words and phrases and is a sort of disclaimer that the reader might be made aware. (It pretty much goes without saying, but one needs to consider that the most important act of God's Creation was man and woman, and everything else that goes along with it. The attitude, then, should be one of joyful appreciation and celebration concerning the rightful and sacred expression of human love in marriage.) The girl is deeply in love with her future husband, the shepherd.

1:3-4—The "Daughters of Jerusalem" consist of Solomon's harem. They come in and take note that the Shulamite girl has been dressed in oils which give forth a sweet-smelling savour and that her name is as pleasant as the oil, meaning that her character is pure. Knowing that she is a favorite with Solomon, they are excited and glad to have her as a member of the harem, trying to entice her to accept King Solomon even though she has been brought there against her will. The girl, however, is still daydreaming about her shepherd lover and wishes that he would come and take her away from where she is—the king's chambers (harem). The women in the harem rightly love (accept) her, recognizing her beauty, and say they will help her with the protocol (probably in dress, manners, etc.) in preparation for the king.

1:5—In her introduction to the harem, she explains that she is "black" but <u>lovely</u> (Heb. *na'veh*= suitable; beautiful) and advises the daughters of Jerusalem that her skin is like the tents of Kedar, 'dusky' (Heb. *qedar*) like those tents, or the curtains (reddish-brown, or olive tanned) in Solomon's palace.

1:6—"Do not keep looking at me," she continues, "it is the deep exposure to the sun which has tanned me." Her color is darker than the light-skinned other maidens in the harem. Her brothers were not quite ready for her to leave home to become the shepherd's wife and gave her the position of looking after the vineyards so that she could give her attention to that and not the shepherd lover. This did not work well as she confesses she did not even take care of her vineyards as she should have.

1:7—Her thoughts go to the shepherd, and wishes she was with him. She daydreams again, wanting to know just where he is, and where does he pasture his flock? Where does he rest in the middle of the day with the flock? "Why can I not be with you instead of being like one who is wandering around and hidden from you?"

1:8—The daughters of Jerusalem interrupt her thoughts, first by agreeing amongst themselves (and with Solomon) that she is surely most beautiful among women. Then they say if she doesn't know where her shepherd is, she should follow the trail of his flock and take up pasturing any goats she has among his and other shepherds.

1:9-10—Solomon begins to woo her. He compares her beauty as being like that of his finest horse. (Beauty was often compared with the best and finest horses in that culture.) He notes that she has excellent facial bone structure with a beautifully smooth neck and suggests that any jewelry to enhance it has to be of the highest quality.

1:11—The rest of the harem, seeing that she pleases Solomon so much, will help prepare her for him and excitedly state they'll make lovely ornaments of the precious gold and silver that he gave for this.

1:12-14—Now she is dining at King Solomon's table as her perfume gives forth fragrance. She has 'fragrance of memories' of her shepherd, which are brought forth by the pouch of myrrh she wears and enables her to stand firm. Like henna blossoms giving forth their protective fragrance to ward off insects from the vineyards, so is the pouch giving her memory of the times spent with her shepherd and helps her to resist Solomon's advances.

1:15—Solomon continues with his wooing and compares her eyes with doves who are known for their beautiful eyes.

1:16-17—The Shulamite girl fixates on the handsomeness of her beloved shepherd. She dreams of their future home for which he is away in the country building for them.

Song of Solomon Commentary 2:1-17

2:1—As the roses respond to the fertility of the valley Sharon, prominent among all of the valleys, so the Shulamite girl responds to memory of her shepherd lover. She considers herself being not special, much like a common rose or crocus which grow profusely in this valley, making it more beautiful than other places. (She may have been speaking this to Solomon, saying in effect that she is only a common girl. This verse is in linguistic feminine gender form, with the next in the masculine.)

2:2—Solomon most probably overheard her speaking to herself (or to the harem maidens, if he did not hear her directly) and picks up on her theme, expressing that she is his most beautiful and greatest love, like a lily growing among thorns, in comparison of all the other women he knows—which number in the hundreds.

2:3—As an apple tree in the forest is beautiful in bloom and useful for nourishment, so is her beloved shepherd among all other men—including Solomon. Under his shadow, or shade (protection) of memories past, she sat down with stability—and his fruit (sustaining words) was "sweet to her taste," or encouraging.

2:4—Being with him is like being in a house of celebration, and his love for her brings strong security. Like a military possession, she is his, and he is hers.

2:5—The Shulamite is so lovesick and missing her shepherd that she admits she needs substance like raisins or apricots and apples to give her strength.

2:6—She looks ahead to a time when she and her shepherd lover can again embrace.

2:7—The Shulamite girl turns to the daughters of Jerusalem and pleads that they do not try to force or stir up love for the King as it, love, comes naturally and will be fulfilled at the proper time—

"*until it pleases*"—with her shepherd lover. (Some translations have the pronoun "she" or "he" in the place of the preposition "it," which in Hebrew is the neutral word *shel*, with no pronoun here. The more accurate translation is, "Do not stir up or awaken love until it pleases." In other words, do not force love upon me for Solomon. My love is for the shepherd in due, or right, time.)

2:8-14—The girl is now dreaming or recalling a time when her shepherd lover ran to meet with her. He ran like a young deer to where she was in her house, stopping at the wall and looking through her window, inviting her to come out and come away with him to spend their precious time together.

2:15—However, her brothers come upon the scene and order her to start the day's work in the vineyards by catching (or scaring away) the little foxes that feed on the young, tender grapes.

2:16-17—She is greatly disappointed, but she knows that she and her shepherd belong to each other. (The idea here is that they are knit together in a true love, soulmate relationship.)

So she encourages him at the right time to come back again on some cool evening with the speed of a stag who roams the mountains of Bether. (Bether, or 'Beter,' is a craggy hill place in Israel, *perhaps* the area where he is building their future home.)

Song of Solomon Commentary 3:1-11

3:1—The Shulamite girl is explaining to the daughters of Jerusalem—the rest of the harem—in the following verses how night after night she had this dream concerning her shepherd lover, or she may be explaining an actual event that took place. If it was only a dream—which it may very well have been—then there is a high probability that she later followed her dream and acted it out, for later she does the same thing, as will be seen.

3:2—She arose out of bed—she actually did this or is dreaming it—and went out into the city desiring to find him, but did not.

3:3—She came across the watchmen making their rounds in the city and asked them if they had seen her shepherd. This does not make sense if she was referring to Solomon, who would surely not be roaming around the city at night. (If a girl from the harem would want to see the King on a matter, she could follow a procedure that would enable her to have an audience with him. Not only that but also harem girls are guarded and would not be allowed out, certainly at night and without an escort.) The Shulamite girl slipped out on her own—or dreamed she did so—and she was fortunate not to be mishandled, which is what happened in her second foray through the city streets. (See *5:7*, which is a more plausible explanation.)

3:4—Apparently, the watchmen had not seen her shepherd; but immediately after her inquiry and leaving them, she found him. She clings to and leads him to her family home, which is outside the city, perhaps not too far from beyond its walls, but certainly in a rural setting with its own vineyards. She leads him into her mother's private room—probably her bedroom—(Heb. *cheder*=innermost private chamber), no doubt for the purpose of speaking to her mother about the seriousness of her relationship with the shepherd. (With all the travel around the city, then to and from her house and sneaking back into the harem, this rises doubt that all of this actually took place, and it may have very well been a dream).

3:5-6—As she is relating this to the harem maidens, she hears the commotion of a large procession coming into the city. She interrupts her speaking in order to repeat her charge to the daughters of Jerusalem, as stated previously, to not stir up or try to awaken a love between her and the King. The procession enters the city among dust-like 'smoke' (Heb. '*ashan* =dust) and the exotic perfumes of a merchant who sells them.

3:7-10—The procession is identified as being Solomon coming into the city traveling in his specially made luxuriant chariot carried and surrounded by sixty bodyguards. The chariot is all decked out not only with the aroma of myrrh and frankincense and other perfumes but also with silver and gold set in purple upholstery, with the interior lovingly fitted, which was done— (Heb.*ratsaph*= embroider; paved) by the daughters of Jerusalem.

3:11—All the women of Jerusalem—literally, Zion (Heb. '*t-siyon-tsee-yone*=Zion-a permanent capital) are encouraged to greet and enjoy King Solomon, who is wearing the crown his mother placed upon him. (He was probably crowned king on the same day of his wedding to Pharaoh's daughter.)

Song of Solomon Commentary 4:1-16

4:1-5—Solomon really pours on the flattery in describing the Shulamite girl's physical attributes. Her eyes are beautiful in color like a dove, the sheen on her hair resembles a flock of goats, strands of which are neatly arranged in unison like goats moving together down the side of Mount Gilead. Her teeth are like bright and newly shorn sheep with none missing (no small thing in those days). Her lips are bright and natural in color, with a well-formed mouth producing beautiful speech. Her forehead is compared to an nicely sliced, well-formed pomegranate with her hair (veil) perfectly framing her face. Her neck has perfect symmetry, much like the Tower of David, referring to strength and dignity. Her breasts are like young twin fawns of a gazelle, beautifully delicate, small, and tender. (Ancient peoples often used their natural surroundings such as animals, architecture, and agriculture in similes and metaphoric phrases to compare with human character, form, and beauty.)

4:6—An exasperated Shulamite girl interrupts Solomon to let him know that she is impervious to his flattery and that she is looking forward to the breaking of **the** day when she can go home with her shepherd lover to his fragrant hills. Myrrh and frankincense produce a 'fragrance of memories'—much like the pouch of myrrh—in remembrance of her shepherd lover. The memories of what have been, and the expectation of what is to come with her shepherd lover, is shielding her from the smooth talk of Solomon as he earnestly continues to woo her over to him.

4:7-11—Solomon pours on the flattery and presses her to come away with him to the many lodgings he no doubt has in various areas. He is telling her that she's the most perfectly beautiful girl he has ever seen. She has "ravished" his heart meaning that she has so much taken hold or captured him that she is an equal like a *"sister"* (a word or expression indicating a very strong feeling akin to the deep affection towards a personal relative); and more than that, he assumes she will soon be his bride. One glance into her eyes sends him reeling. In verse 7 is the phrase "all fair" (Heb. *Kole yapheh—kole-feh-* 'every way—beauty'). In verse 10, the word "fair" (Heb. *yaphah—yaw-faw*—'beauty emanates; brightly shines') introduces a love in his heart, which is the **epitome** of fine taste and elegance (as compared with fine wine and elegant spices).

In fact, her natural body simply greased with olive oil (Heb. *shemen*—olive oil) is not needful of all the spices. Her speech has the purity and sweetness of honey and milk, and her clothes clean and bright as the snows of Mount Lebanon. Her love would be ecstasy to him.

4:12-15—She is a *"garden closed"*—firmly private and for no one else to enjoy, a fountain spring that is sealed up and runs only for the owner. A spring always runs—if it doesn't, it is no longer a spring. Any fountain that doesn't flow can no longer be called a fountain. But, here is pictured a flowing spring bringing forth a fountain of pure water for her soulmate only, which is analogous to the Shulamite girl's firmly held chastity, and for her shepherd, and no one else.

The description of her beauty and yet to be released passion is seen in the comparison with the various delightful fragrances, trees, and fruits. Her youth is compared with living freshwaters, her purity being a large part of her beauty. Solomon spares no enticing verbiage in his attempt to woo this most beautiful and spotless girl for his wife. The best bride—indeed, the only way a bride is supposed to be—is one with no sinful impurities, pure in thought, mind, and body. The Shulamite girl's <u>virginity</u>—(Heb. word for this *"hode,"* which can only be given once, after which it no longer exists)—is vastly important and expressed more than once in *"The Song of Solomon."* (Here is indicated that one can possess 'virginity' of spirit, thought, and mind as well as body.)

4:16—The north wind is to head south to cool Solomon's ardor and then continue south to spread the fragrance of her garden to the shepherd lover, enticing him to come and make it his garden and enjoy its pleasant fruits. Meaning, of course, for the shepherd lover to come for his bride.

Song of Solomon Commentary 5:1-16

5:1—Solomon is still trying to win her over. *"My garden"*— he still thinks that she is going to belong to him, hence the personal pronouns of ownership: *"my garden, my sister, my spouse."* She is going to come to **my** garden and be one of the family like a *"sister"* (as previously explained), and she will be my wife, he reasons. He has gone about preparing a celebration with the aroma of spices and of tasty foods and drink, inviting his friends to eat and drink. The phrase *" I have eaten my honeycomb with my honey"* is an idiom stating that he has had experience in all this (he had other wives). He believes in his arrogance that no girl can resist him for long.

5:2—The Shulamite girl has a very troubled evening (akin to her previous scenario in chapter 3:1-4). She falls asleep, but her heart is awake. The word here for awake (Heb. *oor - 'ur* =to wake up; open the eyes) shows that she awoke from her sleep upon hearing her shepherd lover who is at the door and knocking, asking her to open it up for him. It is raining, and he is getting wet. Notice he does not call her his bride, but rather his *"sister"* (see previous explanation), his love, and not like Solomon, who, in his arrogance, calls her his bride and thinks she is very soon to be his wife. Both Solomon and the shepherd lover in their conversations call her *"sister,"* again meaning the relationship is more than just a friend but close like a member of the family. Solomon wants the relationship with the Shulamite girl to be very close, but it is not, whereas the girl and the shepherd agree that theirs is a very close and intimate love. (This is similar to Christians calling their brethren "brother" and "sister," indicating a closeness of the relationship.)

5:3—She makes excuses to her shepherd lover, which are rather petty. Her response shows that all this is unexpected, and she is somewhat frightened at the timing for it is nighttime, and furthermore, he may be caught and arrested for interfering with the girls of the harem. Is putting on her robe and washing her feet again such a hard task as she makes it out to be? Her excuses further exacerbate her confusion of mind at the suddenness of his appearing.

5:4-5—But her shepherd lover is persistent, and she moves to open the door. Her feelings (Heb. *me-eh* - may-aw; bowels= to be soft of heart) were aroused, and she yearned for him. She arose (Heb. *qum- koom* = 'to rise; get up; rouse up'), and although she could again be dreaming all this, the wording in her state of awakening strongly suggest it is an event that took place. (This is in the past tense, and she is relating—dream or not—an event that recently "happened.") She went to open the door with her hands, which are moist with the bedtime ointments used before bedding down.

5:6—She opened the door, but he was gone, probably because she took so much time to answer, and this late-night intrusion was tenuous at best. She stepped out in search for him and called out, but there was no answer.

5:7—As in her previous event—or "dream" (3:3)—the watchmen of the city found her but left her alone. Now, however, thinking she was probably a woman of the streets, they roughed her up a bit. The keepers of the walls and the watchmen are the same; they bruised her and the taking away of her veil or scarf suggests that she may have been able to literality tear herself away and run back into the harem. If the watchmen knew that she was in the harem, they would not have treated her so as the penalty for interfering or violating a harem in any way was death. And again, if she was enamored of Solomon, she would not be going outside the harem searching for her beloved, someone other than Solomon.

5:8—Now she is fully awake **if** she was dreaming it all; nevertheless she is again saying to the daughters of Jerusalem—the harem—that if they somehow should find or come across him (he might return in his attempt to see her) 'tell him that I am still deeply in love with him.'

5:9—The harem is now **very** curious. Her consistent enthusiasm for a mere shepherd and her continued refusal of love from Solomon puzzles them. Why would anyone reject a king who is tall, handsome, and the richest man in the world for a mere obscure country lad? What is so special about him—especially when compared to a man like Solomon?

5:10—This gives her just the opportunity she wants to explain to the very inquisitive harem why she is so enamored with her shepherd lover. This questioning from the harem would be an absurdity if this beloved in question was Solomon, for is he is known by everyone in the harem, so it makes perfect sense that she is speaking about someone else. The Shulamite uses several metaphors and similes to excitingly describe her beloved's physical appearance and character. She begins by saying he is dazzling bright (Heb. *tsah—sak-h*=white; radiant) and ruggedly handsome (Heb. *adom*—red, as rugged) and stands out among all others. She continues:

5:11—His head is beautiful as pure gold with the hair soft and velvety black.

5:12—His eyes have symmetry, blue as water with the whites as clearest milk and set perfectly in place.

5:13—His cheeks are as fragrant spices with lips that are sweet to the touch—suggesting that they are soft and comfortable to kiss.

5:14—He has attractive hands, strong yet soft and with his abdomen area is perfectly formed, rugged and handsome as jewels, and shows his strength. (Often in Hebrew culture male dress showed a bare midriff, especially among common laborers. In harems such as Solomon's, female dress ofttimes include the bare midriff.)

5:15—His legs are muscular, strong as marble columns set upon solid foundations. His physical appearance is showing that he is as beautiful (handsome) as Mount Lebanon—a prominent snow-capped mountain in Israel—and regal like the cedar trees in that area.[1]

5:16—His mouth is very sweet to kiss, and yes, *"he is altogether lovely"* (Heb. *machmad—mak-mawd* ='delightful, an object of affection or desire'). She finishes the description of her shepherd lover by saying in effect—"This is my beloved and my intimate friend" (Heb. *rea reya* = 'close intimate relationship like family').

---

1 The metaphoric verbiage and phrases so frequently used in *"Songs"* can be traced back to ancient Chaldean and Sumerian languages. From there even to Oriental pictographic linguistic expressions, which is a fascinating study in itself. (See footnote on Appendix title page.)

Song of Solomon Commentary 6:1-13

6:1—So appealing is the testimony of the Shulamite girl for her shepherd lover that the harem desires to meet this 'quintessence of masculinity' and ask where he is that they may seek him as well.

6:2—She answers—rather vaguely—that he is gone to his place—or home—to make it pleasant and to care for his sheep (Heb. *ra-rh* = 'to tend a flock') in the fields while he continues to build for their future. The phrase *"to gather lilies"* (Heb. *laqat shushan-law-kat shoo-shan*) is a common metaphor often used to 'gather' or build something of value—to 'properly align or organize.' He is no doubt fixing up or building a home for them.

6:3—She is stating rather firmly that she needs no help in finding him and emphatically states that they belong to each other—and that's that! He is busily engaged in building for their future.

6:4-7—Solomon comes upon the scene, trying to woo her by complimenting again on her beauty. He speaks in the common middle- eastern imagery that he used earlier (see 4:1-3).

>Tirzah (Heb. *tirtsah*—'*teer-tsaw* =a delight; a city'.)[2]

6:8-10—Here is some idea of the number of Solomon's wives, concubines, and maidens in his immediate harem. But the Shulamite girl is unique, as compared to the women around Solomon in his harem and elsewhere of whom there are so many that they are practically numberless. Evidently, some of these women apprised her and agreed with Solomon that she is indeed

---

2 Tirzah, a city in Ephraim east of Samaria and the north of Shechem, is mentioned in Joshua 12:24 as one of the cities north of Jerusalem that Joshua conquered. Like Jerusalem, it was known for its beautiful setting. Solomon probably built one of his palaces there, and it was the abode of several kings (who were mostly evil), which ruled after him. The word is taken from the Chaldee primary root *ratsah,* meaning 'to be pleased or delighted'; and is also used in simile describing an Israelite girl who is 'bright and beautiful.' It is a compact description of a place or person that appears delightful and beautiful to the eye.

outstanding physically and in all other ways. She was even the most favored one of her mother (most probably because all the other siblings were brothers). They ask who else except this girl is as bright as early morning, fair as the moon, clear as the sun, and awe-inspiring as two large armies in formation and decked out with bright colored banners?

6:11—The Shulamite deflects Solomon's verbosity by recalling the day she went down to a valley close by to see whether the nut trees (most probably walnut trees common in that area) and fruit vines had yet budded.

6:12—Then suddenly, without even understanding what was happening, Solomon came by in his chariot, took her up, and she found herself riding away beside him 'as one having nobility.'

In the Hebrew Scriptures, a more definitive translation into English reads: *"Before I knew it, I found myself in a chariot, and with me was a prince."*[3]

6:13—This is a rather difficult verse as to who is speaking; however, whereas the word *"return"* (come back) in the first part of the verse is expounded on four times, it indicates very serious inflections and therefore gives us the best clue. The Hebrew word is *shub—shoob*= an excited call to 'turn back' or 'reverse,' or even' fetch home again'; therefore, it must be that the friends and family of the Shulamite girl, also wondering what is happening are loudly protesting to what appears to be a kidnapping and not wanting her to be taken from them.

---

3 Scripture quotation was taken from the *Complete Jewish Bible,* Copyright @ 1998 and 2016 by David H, Stern. Used by permission. All rights are reserved worldwide.

The second part of this verse seems to be the Shulamite crying out to Solomon, "What do you want with me, a lowly maiden of the fields? You have the equivalent of two great and colorful armies in the many harem women who serve and perform (dance) for you." Or this could be seen as the village people and her family crying out to bring her back.: 'Why, King Solomon, do you look at her as being as beautiful more than two armies arrayed in splendor?'[4]

This also is the first time that the term "Shulamite" is used in this epistle. It refers to an inhabitant of Shunem (called a Shulamite or Shunammite), a town north of Jerusalem and Tirzah next to the plains of Jezreel. *1 Kings* 1:3-4 records another beautiful girl named Abishag, a "Shunammite" who was brought in to care for King David in his old age. Elisha, the prophet, was administered to with rest and food by a prominent woman as he passed through Shunem (*2 Kings* 4:8-37). Many inhabitants of the town were known for their nobility and prominence in society. (Shunem is now called Salem.)

(This *may* (?) be why Solomon was in the area, known for its beautiful women—looking for a beautiful girl—and he found her!)

---

4 The Hebrew word for "dance" is *m'cloah (meh-o-law)*—meaning a company or unit, and coupled with the Hebrew word *machaneh (makh-an-eh)*= Mahanaim, is a noun meaning 'two hosts' (of angelic origin); or 'an encampment of armies.' The phrase translates into "hosts of angels," the place being named such by Jacob when he witnessed the presence of protective angels as recorded in *Genesis 32:1-2*. The rendering of **two** hosts (or camps) can be understood as either the company Jacob had with him plus the angels that assisted; or angels in such number as being the equivalent of two armies. The event was memorialized later by Hebrews as "The Dance of Two Camps," a celebration which included feasting as well as dancing. Here the "*two camps*" are metaphorically describing the beauty of the Shulamite girl.

Song of Solomon Commentary. 7:1-13

7:1—Solomon continues his exotic phrases in trying to win the Shulamite girl to become his bride as he compares her to various choice majestic cities within his realm, as well as to produce and drink. He lavishes praise on her physical appearance, starting with her feet up to her head, then down to her breasts again and back up, ending with her facial features.

"How beautiful are your feet in sandals…" (Heb. *pa-am, pa-amah—pah-am*=feet; footsteps). She is clothed in shoes or sandals that are delicate and probably brightly colored to enhance the beauty of the feet, thereby producing 'dainty' footsteps. It was very common for ancient women in the beautifying of their physical appearance to pay special attention to their feet and dress them in beautiful, well-shaped slippers or sandal-like shoes, often well- jeweled. He thinks she is spectacular in her beauty and has the grace of a nobleman's daughter—rich looking, elegant, well-poised and graceful, with the symmetry of her body like the beautiful work of an artist.

*"The curves (*joints) *of your thighs are like jewels…"* (Heb. *chammuq-kham-mook* = 'wrapping'; 'rounded'—*yarek yaw-rake*='thigh; hip.') Her hips are well-rounded like a skilled jeweler would 'round' and fit precious stones in their setting. This was considered to be one of the most attractive parts of a female's anatomy, especially when combined with a well-shaped (and dressed) foot.

7:2-9a—The next several verses continue Solomon's comparisons, some of which are repeats of his earlier erotic praises. Solomon confesses that the Shulamite's beautiful physical appearance with stature (posture) like a palm tree (Heb. *tamar—taw-mar'* -'to be erect like a palm') has captivated him. He compliments more than once her well-shaped breasts **(4:5).**

In fact, as his future wife, he looks forward to embracing her in lovemaking (**7:8a).**

7:9b-10—And so as Solomon continues verbalizing his erotically romantic list of various compliments—some of which she has heard before—the Shulamite interrupts to let him know in no uncertain terms again that she loves someone else and not him. Yes, the wine goes down smoothly through her lips to the man she loves—him (the shepherd), not you—and awakens his love. "I belong to my beloved man, and he desires and belongs to me."

7:11-13—*"Come, my beloved, let us go forth..."* (Heb. *halak-haw-lak*='to walk, go forward'; to 'run along, to come along') and *'go forth'* (Heb. *yatsa* = 'to go out'; 'escape'). These two phrases are in future tense and, as such, reveal that the girl is thinking ahead to when the time is right for their marriage when she can give herself to her shepherd lover. All along, she has resisted the charms of Solomon and saved her love, which is like the sweet taste of the fresh fruits for her shepherd.

The phrase **"...*new and old...*"** *(13)* refers to her love for the shepherd, which she has carried for some time, probably when she was much younger, up to the present. This gives a strong indication of a genuine 'soulmate' love between the the two.[5]

---

5 *Songs"* throughout uses *erotic* words and phrases (as so considered within our culture) in describing the Shulamite girl and even the shepherd lover. This is one of the reasons why many skip over *"Songs"* and only use carefully chosen phrases or words which are less "erotic" and are therefore deemed to be "safe" for use. The Bible, however, is very straightforward and "doesn't pull punches," as we might say in our culture. The Scriptures must be understood and interpreted within the background of their ancient cultures and not as much in accordance with our modern Western society. This can make it difficult to correctly discover real meanings and thoughts behind certain phrases and scenarios in various scriptural passages unless we adhere to these ancient cultures. Certain metaphors and similes that are used by these ancient languages in comparisons and descriptions, which would be considered to be very 'vulgar' and 'distasteful' in our modern culture, would not necessarily be thought so in ancient times. This difference in conceptual semantics can be seen even in the development of our own English language when comparison

is made between Elizabethan or Middle-age English with the modern. For example, the culture of the language in 1611 from which the King James Bible originated accepted the way of referring to males as did ancient Hebrew society. (Examples can be seen in the KJV Bible in the following verses: *1 Samuel 25:22,34; 2 Kings 18:27; Isaiah 36:12*, to name a few.) Certain phrases and words were not considered vulgarities back in the 17th century as they would be now. Modern versions of the Bible have sought to lessen the shock of such verses with more acceptable terminology, but the effect that God means to convey is still clearly evident. And the whole chapter of *Ezekiel 23* gives a vivid analogy of the spiritual harlotry in Judah and Israel in using—what we would consider—harsh graphic language describing two very wicked adulterous sisters, which would no doubt be given in X-rating in our society today. As we might express in our culture, the Bible does not "pussy-foot around."

Song of Solomon Commentary 8:1-14

8:1-2—The Shulamite girl's wishful thinking continues on, hoping that the relationship with her shepherd would be accepted by the people in her village like a relationship between brothers and sisters. (It was common to use the family term 'brother' and 'sister' in referring to one deeply loved, as previously mentioned. Solomon called the Shulamite girl 'sister' more than once.) Then she could kiss him and would not be despised or thought ill of, and have light conversation with her mother as she gives him juice to drink from the fruits of her own garden. And everything would be in proper order. In fact, the phrase *"juice of my pomegranate"* is in idiom, indicating in the context of the scenario she is describing that the setting is proper. In Hebrew, the word *juice* is *min minniy minney -min, min-nee', min-n*ay'= 'properly a part of'; hence (prepositionally) from or out of. The rest of the phrase with the word *"my"* is a possessive determiner, showing that the Shulamite girl is the owner or originator of this physical fruit, equating her love for the shepherd to be as delectable as the taste of this delicious fruit.

8:3-4—She envisions herself in the arms of her beloved and then turns to address the harem more sternly than before, and for the last time, says not to try and turn her love to Solomon.

(Heb. *shaba - shaw-ba*k ='to seriously charge'; 'promise'; 'take an oath.') She leaves out speaking the soft and tender metaphor of the gazelles and deer that she included before (**2:7; 3:5**). She's very determined that the harem understands her love can **never** be for Solomon!

8:5—Solomon finally gives in and allows the girl to go back home. The shepherd lover comes for her and is bringing her there in his wagon. At first, the village people wonder who this is. The girl confirms that this was where she was born, and the shepherd confirms this is where he met her and fell in love. The apple tree is symbolic of the home. *"I awakened you under the apple tree"* or *"I raised you up"* is a metaphor illustrating their recognition or awareness of their love. (Heb. *'uwr* -oor =‘opening the eyes’; ‘wake’; ‘stir up.’)

8:6—Pledging themselves to each other, she accepts his "engagement ring"—(Heb. *chatham*-=‘seal’; ‘signet’; ‘ring’). It was common practice in Hebrew society to wear a type of locket next to the heart with the name or portrait of a family member or loved one engraved on it. *"Seal upon the arm"* refers to the closeness of the relationship by strongly embracing each other.

The Shulamite girl speaks on in expressing the deepness and strength of her love for her shepherd by several similes: *"strong as death"*—(permanent); *"jealousy cruel as the grave"* (inexorable zeal, impossible to stop); *"coals of fire, a "most vehement flame"*-(Heb. *yahh* -yaw-h - *yah*:= conjunction of Yahweh, the name of God, as most vehement—‘forceful’; ‘strongly passionate’). This last phrase could be literally interpreted *"fierce as the flame of God (Yah),"* the only time the name of the Lord is used in *"The Song of Solomon."* These verses illustrate that there is nothing that can suppress or overcome the power and reality of genuine love.

8:7—True, real love cannot be extinguished. Love is like the "flame of God" when the prophet Elijah called upon God, who then sent fire, which consumed his water-soaked sacrifice and *"licked up the water that was in the trench"* (*1 Kings 18:37-38*). The latter part of this verse reveals the futility of building one's love on material things.

8:8-9—Now her brothers speak, using Hebrew idioms. They review their sister's childhood—(*"she has no breasts"*- Heb. *ayin* = ‘has not’; ‘to be nothing’; a ‘non-entity’—an idiom describing a young female child), and then they discuss what they will do for her when the day comes that she is ready for marriage. If she has remained a virgin (*"a wall"*-Heb. *chomah -kho-maw* -fem. active=‘a wall of protection’; ‘private estate’), then they will present her with a dowry. If she has not remained virtuous but is otherwise (*"a door"*- (Heb. *deleth -deh'leth*=‘a swinging gate’; ‘door’; ‘entrance for others’), they will disavow her. When they mention enclosing her with boards, they seem to be speaking, as it were, tongue-in-cheek, for this is an extreme action to take.

However, knowing the intense temptations of being with a king, especially one like Solomon, what they are saying rings with an inquisitive tone as to whether she did stay true and virtuous for her shepherd while incarcerated in Solomon's harem.

8:10—She reaffirms to her brothers that she is a wall, a developed chaste woman staying true to her beloved shepherd, and has brought favor and peace to him in knowing that she is his pure soulmate. In expressing her anatomy—*"my breasts like towers"*—(Heb. *migdalah—mig-daw-law*=‘as a high tower’; ‘bed of flowers’), she is applying an idiom comparing herself like the tower of God (Heb. *Migdal-'el*)—a special and reserved place; meaning, of course, she is only for her shepherd lover.

8:11-12—She speaks of Solomon's vineyards in a place called ‘Baal Hamon,’ where he leased land to workers, which increased his riches, thereby helping to make him a very desirable person of wealth. The Shulamite girl was not interested and fended off his romantic advances. She had her own vineyard—her shepherd lover. She had just alluded to the fact that wealth, or money, can't buy love (cf. *8:7*).

8:13-14—In the presence of all the witnesses around who are listening for him to proclaim her as his bride, she requests her shepherd lover make it loud and clear with celerity, like a gazelle or a young deer.

Thus ends a beautiful love story that concludes with the triumph of purity in real and true love over the allurements of temptations.

ELEVEN

Why "*Songs*" is
Important For Our Edification

1. This "Song of Songs" is considered the best of the 1000+ songs that Solomon wrote. It is recognized—or should be—as a celebration of the holiness and beauty of human love within the sanctity of Biblical marriage.

2. Backed up with statements in his other writings, a clearer picture and understanding of the man Solomon is developed.

3. The erotic imagery of songs shows God's approval of such eroticism within the context of lawful marriage.

4. "*Songs*" can be thought of as a beautiful analogy of the love between God and the believer (or Church).

5. "*Songs*" easily lends itself to Christian analogy where Solomon represents the world, the Shulamite girl the Christian (and/or church), with the shepherd lover the Lord Jesus Christ. In representing Christ, the shepherd lover is our Savior who is away preparing a place to dwell with his bride the Church, and in the end times returning to consummate their marriage (*John 14:2-3*).

(It should be remembered that any analogy to Christ is not Hebraic for the church was a "mystery" until it was revealed in the New Testament: *(Romans 16:25*; *Ephesians 3:1-11, 6:19; Colossians 1:24-27.* That being said, however, we need to also remember that the Old Testament foreshadows just about all that the New Testament reveals and is a necessary background and compliment to the New.)

6. Finally, human love and marriage as ordained by God and being an extremely important—if not the most important—element of Creation must be practiced with utmost honor and respect, and done so according to God's direction and principles. *"Songs"* gives us an example of such in the Shulamite girl's steadfast focus and concentration on the man destined to be her husband. She was able to stand firm against the strong temptations hurled at her. Emboldened by the earnest love of her soulmate to be, she was resolute in waiting for him to come for her. Her brothers, recognizing her assertiveness and victory over the extremely overwhelming circumstances and temptations, were able to honor her with a rich dowery (*Songs 8:9*a). She did not succumb to another man who was, in the worldly sense, "a catch"—tall, handsome, very rich, and positioned famously high in society. She believed, as Solomon finally discovered, that true happiness and fulfilled satisfaction in life is the soulmate from God and the application of God's principles in proper worship of the Creator. (Review in this order: *Ecclesiastes 9:9; Proverbs 5;18-19; Ecclesiastes 12:1, 6-7.*)

TWELVE

Summary and Conclusions

Solomon, the author of three Biblical books—*Proverbs, Ecclesiastes,* and *The Song of Solomon*, in his writings reveal many 'gems,' of the wisdom he received from God. They also reveal a look at his character and life. In character, he was a humble and truthful man, as evidenced by (1) his request to God when told whatever he wanted would be granted and his only desire was to be able to rule wisely for his people; (2) and when he confessed to his failures in his personal life. He wrote of his mother Bathsheba's concern of two of his most blatant weaknesses—women and drink *(Proverbs 31:1-5)*. He evidently resolved any alcohol problem he may have had but fell prey to his womanizing. Much of the advice in *Proverbs* that he addressed to young men were the dangers of promiscuity. An example of such is where he seems to reflect back on his failure to heed advice and instruction when he was a young man, and in effect, is saying, "Don't do what I did" (*Proverbs 5:13-14*). Solomon concludes his proverbial essay by describing the ideal wife (*Proverbs 13:10-31*). This is something that every woman should strive to be. It is not something a person cannot achieve and is not to be an elite, perfect, or "snobbish" or anything like that, but a goal, or character traits, to develop in life.

Hebrews 13:4 states that *"Marriage is honorable among all…"* meaning that marriage is to be held in honor by everyone. In this day and age, our culture—our society—is abandoning our Creator God and His precepts and principles, which is especially true among the youth with their self-centered, cavalier attitude. The chapters on love and marriage seek to bring out a deeper understanding on the truths of these subjects and the necessity of holding these concepts in a much more honorable position than is evident in today's world. Solomon's failures in these areas pinpoint the frustration and misery that occur in a person's life when Godly principles in love and marriage (and in other areas as well) are ignored.

In "*Songs,*" Solomon courts a young woman who he believes is to be his special wife. Solomon, through his many women, was led away by them from God and went along with them in the worship of pagan gods. God's anger, because of this, caused the split of the kingdom after his death. His failure in achieving satisfaction concerning this highest and most precious reward in life (*Ecclesiastes 9:9*) colored all other areas in his life. It helped lead him to the truth as described in the closing statement of his humble confession: *"Let us hear the conclusion of the matter: Fear God and keep His commandments, for this is man's all. For God will bring every work into judgment, including every secret thing, whether good or evil" (Ecclesiastes 12:13-14).* In this final statement (most probably written in his old age), Solomon is revealing the highest and best of all his wisdom. God created the universe and everything in it, all forms of life, including mankind, His supreme creation. The commandments Solomon speaks of is the Word of God—given for our knowledge of Him and our guidance in this life. We would do well to heed Solomon—the wisest man of all, save for the Lord Himself—as he gives forth his last "gem" of wisdom, which in effect is telling us that a life lived without God is no life at all.

God, in His supreme love of mankind, came to earth as a man to rescue His beloved creation from the domain of the devil. His death on the cross provides the way for man to have eternal life with Him. We cannot have this through **any** human activity or event. *"For by grace you have been saved through faith, and that not of yourselves; it is the gift of God, not of works lest anyone should boast" (Ephesians 2:8-9).* It is a **gift** of God through His fathomless love, grace, and mercy. We cannot gain the favor of God for salvation by good works, religious ceremonies or activity, or anything else conceived by the human mind and spirit. God has done it all, and we cannot add anything to it. *"But we are all like an unclean thing, and all our righteousnesses are like the filthy rags; we all fade as a leaf, and our iniquities, like the wind, have taken us away" (Isaiah 64:6);* and *"For whoever calls on the name of the Lord shall be saved" (Romans 10:13;* cf. *John 3:16).* Upon believing and receiving Jesus Christ as Lord and Savior, we are then called to do good works according to Godly principles, and in this, we will have reward in the next life—which, by the way, is the only **real** life.

Saved—from what? From an eternity existing in a region called Hell. Many people ridicule and do not believe that there is a Hell, but just because they say that does not mean that Hell does not exist. It surely does exist. Jesus himself spoke of Hell's existence many times (*Matthew 5:22,29,30; 10:28; 11:23,* etc*)*. When God created man, he created him in **His image**. The image of God cannot die. The image of God is eternal. It cannot be extinguished, and when Adam, the first man, disobeyed God, his commitment and dominion over Creation 'slipped' into the devil's control, who is the *prince* of the power of the air, the ruler of the earth. God allows this in order that freedom of choice for mankind can exist but did set some boundaries, as seen in the opening verses of the book of *Job*. Jesus Christ will redeem his Creation and return to earth in the near future to rule as Creation's righteous King. He is not willing that any should perish: (*"The Lord is not slack concerning his promise, as some count slackness, but is long* *suffering toward us, not willing that any should perish but that all should come to repentance" (2 Peter 3:9).* God blessed mankind with the precious and wonderful but recalcitrant gift—free will. Otherwise, we would be like robots. God doesn't send anyone to hell; a person's free will does—it is his or her choice.

As for those who don't believe God or His Word—the wisdom of the Scriptures state: *"The fool has said in his heart, "There is no God."(Psalm 14:1a*-and repeated in *Psalm 53:1a).*

Any human wisdom, truth, or principle that is not from or based upon God's truth and principles, as found in his word, is in error. Solomon surely discovered in his *Ecclesiastes* confessional that this life is "vanity," and the next with God is the only worthwhile and true life.

Hear again the best wisdom for anyone wishing to be blessed with a successful and happy life, now and forever, from the wisest man (apart from Jesus Christ) that ever walked the Earth: *"For the Lord gives wisdom; from His mouth comes knowledge and understanding; He stores up sound wisdom for the upright; He is a shield to those who walk uprightly (in integrity)"(Proverbs 2:6-7).*

And that's *"the conclusion of the matter"*!

APPENDIX

The following chart is a detailed explanation of the Hebrew alphabet.

The top of the block in each row shows the written form of the letter. Next to the letter on the right side is the number, which each letter represents when numerics are called for. (Hebrew is read from right to left. Its alphabet contains 22 letters, all consonants; vowel signs are *'jots'* and *'tittles'* > (. ').

Below each letter and number is the *transcription* (sound) of the letter (spelled out in English phonetics). Sometimes the transcription may vary in spelling; examples are: *beth* for *beyt, daleth* for *dalet, he* for *hey,* etc.

Next, below the transcription is the Paleao-Hebrew (Chaldee; sometimes Sumerian) *pictograph*—a "picture" of the central object, feeling, or action meant by the letter.[1]

---

1 *The Sumerians had one of the oldest written languages (Semitic). They invented cuneiform writing, wedge-shaped characters which were used in the Paleolithic (ancient) writings of Mesopotamia, Persia, and also Ugarit—a language dialect named after a large ancient port and merchandising city in northern Syria. The Chaldean basic language (Chaldee) was Semitic. Aramaic is a Syrian Semitic dialect being formed about the 6th century BC. Both Chaldean language and Aramaic dialect blended into the forming of the Paleolithic Semitic Hebrew, and soon Aramaic developed along with the Paleo-Hebrew and was itself reformed into Arabic in 7AD. The man used by God to begin the Hebrew nation was a Chaldean named Abram (from Ur of the Chaldees- Genesis 11:31). The language Abram (Abraham) spoke was no doubt, Semitic- Chaldee. The development of Hebrew from basically the Semitic- Chaldee came after Abraham. (Later, the Aramaic dialect strengthened into the Arabic language written and spoken by many nomadic tribes in the area.) The name "Hebrew" is a Chaldee-Hebrew phrase from the Aramaic root word 'ibray, meaning "one who crosses over—i.e., 'the river.' "*

Finally, the bottom words in the specific block continue to explain what the letter through the pictograph communicates— i.e., an object, feeling, action, or a combination of such.

A letter's particular meaning is controlled by the **context** of the phrase, sentence, or paragraph of which it is a part.

Vav 6	Hey 5	Dalet 4	Gimel 3	Beyt 2	Alef 1
Nail Secure Add/and	Behold Reveal Breath	Door Move Entrance	Foot Camel Pride	House Family in	Ox Strength Leader
Lamed 30	Kaf 20	Yod 10	Tet 9	Chet 8	Zayin 7
Shepherd Staff/Teach To/from	Palm To open Allow/tame	Arm/hand Work/deed Worship	Basket Snake Surround	Wall Fence Separation	Plow Weapon Cut off
Tsade 90	Pev 80	Ayin 70	Samekh 60	Nun 50	Mem 40
Man on side Journey Desire/need	Mouth Speak Scatter	Eye Watch Experience	Thorn Support Protect	Seed Fish/life Continue	Water Chaos Blood
Tav 400	Shin 300	Resh 200	Qof 100		
Cross Mark/sign Covenant	Teeth Press/destroy Separate	Head Authority First	Sun Behind Time		

Author's Bibliography

Dr. Ron Surels holds five degrees, including two Masters' and a Ph.D., in the disciplines of education, psychology, theology, Biblical and ancient languages along with a detailed study on the creation of man and woman in Genesis. His life experiences include youth and senior pastor, founder and developer of Christian day schools, college professor, and professional counselor. He is a Korean War veteran of the United States Air Force. Upon discharge, he became a chaplain and liaison officer for the US Army Nike Missile Test Site in the Pacific Kwajalein Atoll. While stationed there, he also helped develop an adult education program in the Marshall Islands for the University of Hawaii. With his wife Lynne, Dr. Ron has served as missionary assistants in South Africa, developing and presenting family seminars and other missionary churches' ministries. His main hobby is researching and writing on history and Biblical themes.

Dr. Surels previously published a book in 1993 dealing with the World War II adventures of a destroyer that was sunk by kamikazes off Okinawa. An oral history from the surviving crew and families of crew members' testimonies, the book was on the US Naval Academy's bestseller list for two years and has gone through two editions.

He and his wife are the parents of three grown and married children. Ron and Lynne reside in rural New Hampshire.